On Toast

On Toast

Tartines, Crostini, and Open-Faced Sandwiches

Kristan Raines

Quarto is the authority on a wide range of topics.

Quarto educates, entertains and enriches the lives of our readers—enthusiasts and lovers of hands-on living.

www.QuartoKnows.com

First published in the United States of America in 2016 by Quarry Books, an imprint of Quarto Publishing Group USA Inc. 100 Cummings Center
Suite 406-L
Beverly, Massachusetts 01915-6101
Telephone: (978) 282-9590
Fax: (978) 283-2742
QuartoKnows.com
Visit our blogs at QuartoKnows.com

10 9 8 7 6 5 4 3 2 1

ISBN: 978-1-63159-077-1
Digital edition published in 2016
eISBN: 978-1-62788-839-4

Library of Congress Cataloging-in-Publication Data
Raines, Kristan, author.
  Toast : tartine, crostini, and open-faced sandwiches / Kristan Raines.
    pages cm
  ISBN 978-1-63159-077-1 (hardback) --
ISBN 978-1-62788-839-4 (digital edition)
1. Toast (Bread) I. Title.
  TX769.R285 2015
  641.81'5--dc23
                                   2015025886

Design: Timothy Samara
Cover Image: Kristan Raines

Printed in China

To my beloved husband John.
Thank you for your love, encouragement,
and endless support.

Contents

Everything that is wrong with our culture begins with the book you hold in your hands.

The epic fetishism and highly focused gourmet-ification of everything under the sun, of which we are all now a part—ice cream, chocolate, coffee, toast, organic, cage-free donut holes—has some frightening aspects and important historical antecedents you should be aware of. Theodor Adorno called it "the culture industry."

The culture industry includes up-selling common items and doubling their price through desire and hypnosis. In terms of marketing "tastes," people today have more access to higher-quality foods than royalty did 200 years ago. This unprecedented demand for the consumption of specialty items as a lifestyle by more and more people means that the planet is dying.

How does this relate to toast?

Toast is a simple food, accessible to all. It is the stuff of peasants and farmers and the earth. It is comfort and nourishment, plain and simple. Somehow, strangely though, it too has become momentarily elevated to the gourmet platform, another shiny object in the pantheon of shiny objects.

Toast is here for a reason, though. It has an ulterior motive.

While this simple food has your attention, here is what toast is really trying to say to you. Here is what it wants you to know:

About 50 percent of people who have a near-death experience get divorced.

That's right. Not what you were expecting to hear? I know, but that's what toast has to say.

Additionally, it wants us to know that helping others is a good use of our time.

I was asked to write this foreword because people have decided that I am one of the people who have heralded the "elevation of toast" to its new status.

In 2007 I opened a café called Trouble Coffee with $1000 and the help of everyone I knew. A community of people gathered to put up drywall, fix old machinery, and build cabinets in a tiny space that became Trouble Coffee. Our motto is "Build Your Own Damn House." We serve coffee, whole coconuts, and toast. Toast was something I grew up with. It's a comfort food.

Less comfortable was an experience when I nearly drowned last year. I have been an ocean swimmer for about eleven years, a practice that helps me shock the illusions out of my system. On this particular day I lost consciousness under the water, pinned against the rocks by a series of rogue waves that were literally pounding me into oblivion. It was only because someone helped me, risking their own life to save mine, that I found myself on the beach, lungs full of water, as I let the ocean out and began to breathe again.

The world is full of people who need our help. This is a good use of our time.

People who come back from near-death experiences commonly report on their change of perspective and also the utter silliness of our various pursuits, spending sprees, and "tastes" that do nothing to help anyone.

After undergoing a near-death experience, it is common for their partners, the people who married them and thought they knew them, to report that their husbands and wives—career-driven, money-making, iron-clad stalwarts—suddenly become almost unknown to them and "just want to help people."

Drowning was the best thing that ever happened to me. I highly recommend it. It is my wish, and that of toast itself, that you too have an experience by which you become who you really are, and unknown to those around you.

Wishing you the best,

—Giulietta Carelli
Founder, Trouble Coffee

P.S. A special thanks goes to Kristan for sharing her love of simple foods, including toast. A need to make toast for others, in all its varieties, started with our own experience as children. To this day there is a magic wonder that goes with a proper toast.

Each Saturday morning my father would wake me up at sunrise and whisk me away to our favorite breakfast spot. We were beyond regulars—I swear our orders were being prepared the moment we walked through the door. My father would have eggs sunny side up with a side of bacon, and I never wanted to grow out of a Belgian waffle with whipped cream. But the most enjoyable part of the morning meal was always my trusty side of sourdough toast, smothered in melted butter and topped with good old-fashioned strawberry jam. It might be hard to believe, but those four little slices of toast brought me so much joy, no matter how full I was.

I know what you're thinking: *Can toast really be that important?* Is it not just a complement to a meal, even an afterthought? Well, I think it can be more, and over the years, I have grown to appreciate how versatile a slice of toast can truly be. Actually, if you think about it for a moment, many of our most beloved meals are simply a slice of toast or a biscuit put to its greatest use, such as eggs Benedict or, of course, French toast. So while fine artisan toast is more likely to be found on cozy breakfast tables and pioneering menus today, it has actually been around for quite some time. Ambitious toast recipes have been gaining popularity, but the idea of dressing a piece of grilled toast for a meal is one of history.

If you think about it for a moment, many of our most beloved meals are simply a slice of toast or a biscuit put to its greatest use, such as Eggs Benedict or, of course, French toast.

Although it might have different names around the world, the idea behind this meal is the same: a slice of bread put to the flame and adorned with delicious toppings. In Scandinavia, for example, you will find a poplar dish called *smørrebrød*. This is traditionally a piece of dark brown bread, like rye, covered with different spreads, cheeses, meats, or fish. And in France, a slice of toast covered with fine ingredients, essentially an open-faced sandwich, is called a tartine. I will always remember the first time I went to Paris, where I had a very popular tartine, the croque monsieur. I loved the fresh ham, the melted Gruyère, the rich béchamel; and this was all crafted out of a slice of toast. So although I love the essential approach that includes just butter and jam, I also think that toast can actually hold the weight of providing a genuinely satisfying meal. That's why I've written this book.

I have a passion for coming up with great ideas and using produce that's in season, and so I have carried this mind-set into creating each recipe. I have divided all the recipes among the four seasons, so that there is a unique approach according to what is naturally yielded during that time. It is my hope that you will be inspired to go out and search through your local farmers' market to find fresh produce at the peak of its season. It is not as though you ought to avoid certain produce if it is unavailable, but rather that you should be inspired to explore what *is* in season and let that guide the development of your meals. Sure, a strawberry can taste good during the fall, but few things can compare to the flavor of biting into a fresh, juicy, perfect red strawberry in the prime of its season.

I have set out to refresh and reimagine the way we use toast so as to make it a source of creating wonderful meals. The result is 100 inventive ways to prepare delicious meals with only a slice of bread as your foundation. So whether you want ricotta cheese, figs, and honey, or smoked salmon and fennel, or just a simple combination of compote and cream, these recipes will allow you to explore the flavors toast can offer in a whole new way.

Ingredients and Techniques

Types of Bread

In the spirit of making the most out of toast, we have to remember how important it is to choose the right type of bread. Be it a loaf of white bread from the market down the street or a rustic loaf from your own oven, the bottom line is that the bread is just as important as everything you put on it. Local bakeries are the ideal place to purchase your bread, as it is in its freshest and most intentional form, but, of course, the bread available at your local stores will work for any of these recipes. Breads are fashioned in many styles, which means they also vary in size. Just remember that this might affect the serving sizes for each toast, along with the recommended amounts of spread, ever so slightly.

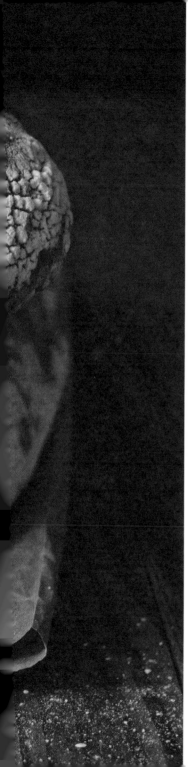

Artisan Bread

Handcrafted rather than mass-produced, artisan bread is enveloped in a beautiful exterior crust and suffused with dynamic flavor. Naturally at home in local bakeries and farmers' markets, artisan bread is forged with meticulous care and furnishes the most rewarding experience for enjoying toast. These loaves are occasionally unsliced, allowing you to determine the thickness of each slice—slices anywhere from ¼ inch to ½ inch (6 to 13 mm) work wonderfully. Use a serrated knife to ensure easy cutting. With artisan bread's intricate, textured exterior and rich, delicate interior, there exists no more exceptional place than this from which to begin your toasting endeavors.

Classic Sandwich Bread

This is the bread that lies close to all our hearts; it is the foundation of our peanut butter and jellies of countless days past and so much more. It's available everywhere and works with all of my recipes, though thicker bread is admittedly more suitable for heartier toppings. This domain is also more desirable when the boundaries of white bread are traversed, so be sure to try whole wheat, rye, squaw, sourdough, and all the other great options these loaves have to offer.

Pantry

Butter

I'd believe it if you found it difficult to imagine making a piece of toast without butter. This is because it imparts such a universally delicious flavor to any slice of bread. Whenever you want that flavor, feel free to add butter to any of the recipes. I suggest using softened unsalted butter, so as to retain that great buttery taste without excessively competing with other flavors on the toast. Spread it with a brush or a knife, just as long as you get a nice layer of butter on each side.

Grapeseed and Olive Oil

Grapeseed and olive oil, like butter, can provide a delightful taste to any toast. Grapeseed oil is a wonderful choice due to its neutral flavor, while olive oil possesses a much more distinct flavor. There is also a variety of other infused oils from which you can choose if you want to introduce another flavor to your toast.

Toasting Nuts

Many of the recipes in this book call for some type of toasted nut because I find that preparing them in this manner really enhances their flavor. To toast your nuts, simply set a skillet over medium-high heat and scatter the nuts in a single layer. Time will vary for different nuts, so simply cook, stirring often, until they become fragrant and have browned a bit. Remove from the pan until ready to use.

Finishing Salts

There exists a plethora of unique finishing salts, all of which are able to contribute another dimension of flavor to any of these toast recipes. Some of my personal favorites include Maldon sea salt, fleur de sel, and Hawaiian sea salt. Your choices are practically endless, so simply find some that you enjoy and experiment with them.

Toasting Techniques

Skillet

This is always a trusty way to prepare a slice of toast. Brush the bread with an even layer of oil or butter and toast over medium heat until golden brown, about 2 to 3 minutes on each side.

Oven

Using your oven is another great way to prepare your toast, especially because you can make multiple slices at once. Preheat the oven to 350°F (180°C, or gas mark 4), brush the bread evenly with oil or butter, and bake for 10 to 12 minutes or until toasted to your liking.

Broiler

Using your oven's broiler is another quick and easy way to toast multiple slices of bread at the same time. Simply place bread that has been brushed with oil or butter onto a baking sheet and place directly under the broiler. Toast each side for about 2 minutes or until toasted to your liking. Keep a constant eye on when using this method as the bread tends to toast quite quickly.

Grill

Grilling a slice of bread over an open fire is a great way to impart a nice char and smoky flavor to your toast; a grill pan will also do the trick. Brush each side of the bread with oil or butter and grill each side for 2 to 3 minutes or until lightly charred on both sides.

Toaster

This, of course, is the classic way to prepare toast and it's especially great when you want a dry slice of toast. Any kind of bread finds a comfortable home in a toaster, so use whatever fits and toast to your liking, buttering afterwards if you wish.

Only durable fruits and vegetables make their appearance during this time of year. Dark leafy greens, earthy root vegetables, and bright citrus fruits are among the amazing produce that can be found at the markets. With a little creativity, much of what this season yields can become a perfect complement to toast.

Recipes for

Winter

Persimmons
and Honeyed Ricotta

———

When I was growing up, my family's neighbor would let us pick our fill of persimmons from their tree each winter. Usually, we would cut off their tops and eat them with a spoon, but little did I know how good these fruits would taste on toast! The natural honey flavors of the fruit come out alongside the sweetened ricotta cheese to make a very tasty meal.

3 tablespoons (48 g) ricotta cheese

1 teaspoon honey, plus more for drizzling

Pinch of salt

1 slice of wheat bread

½ of a medium persimmon, thinly sliced

1 tablespoon (8 g) chopped walnuts, toasted

In a small bowl, mix together the ricotta cheese, honey, and salt; set aside.

Toast the bread to your liking and spread the ricotta cheese mixture over the top.

Place the sliced persimmon on top and sprinkle with the chopped walnuts and a light drizzle of honey.

Yield: 1 serving

Tip

Bee pollen possesses many health benefits and works really well as an added garnish to this recipe.

Apples and Cookie Butter

Luckily, apple season lasts all the way through early winter. This is great because I like having fresh apples on hand, especially when I'm craving cookie butter. I mean, who doesn't like this stuff? It might be a bit dangerous to keep in my kitchen, but it's always worth it when I can pair it with some tart apples for an easy snack.

1 slice of wheat bread

1 to 2 tablespoons (15 to 30 g) cookie butter

4 or 5 thin slices green apple

Honey, for drizzling

1 teaspoon bee pollen, for garnish (optional)

Toast the bread to your liking and then spread a layer of cookie butter over the top. Layer the toast with enough sliced apples to cover. Garnish with a light drizzle of honey and a sprinkle of bee pollen.

Yield: 1 serving

Blood Oranges and Honeyed Ricotta

—

I first heard about blood oranges a few years back, and each winter I look forward to their arrival in the markets. Their distinctive, jewel-like color is complemented by a rich citrus flavor, making them a wonderful addition to many meals. For this recipe, I decided to bring this bright and lovely fruit together with honey-sweetened ricotta cheese and layer them on a nice thick slice of bread.

3 tablespoons (48 g) ricotta cheese

1 teaspoon honey, or more to taste

Pinch of salt

1 slice of honey wheat bread

1 blood orange, peeled and sliced

1 to 2 tablespoons (11 to 22 g) pomegranate seeds

1 teaspoon cocoa nibs

In a small bowl, mix together the ricotta cheese, honey, and salt; set aside.

Toast the bread to your liking and spread a layer of ricotta cheese over the toast. Place the blood orange slices over the top and sprinkle with the pomegranate seeds and a few cocoa nibs.

Yield: 1 serving

Tip

This recipe can easily be turned into a sweet snack; simply add some seasonal fruit or jam.

Fresh Ricotta and Olive Oil

Fresh ricotta cheese on toast may sound simple, but each bite will convince you otherwise. I urge you to source the highest quality ingredients for this recipe, as this is really what makes it taste so good! Also, try to get your hands on some thick slices of bread, as it provides a sturdy foundation for all that delicious ricotta cheese.

1 slice of spelt sour-dough bread

3 tablespoons (48 g) fresh ricotta cheese

Olive oil, for drizzling

Pink Himalayan salt, to taste

Toast the bread to your liking and spread a layer of fresh ricotta cheese over the top. Drizzle with a bit of olive oil, adding pink Himalayan salt to taste.

Yield: 1 serving

Sausage and Egg Tartine

Nothing will get me out of bed faster than a cup of freshly brewed coffee and the pleasing aroma of sizzling sausage. And while I usually make fairly simple breakfasts, sometimes I like to indulge. So an open-faced breakfast sandwich like this, filled with all my favorite things, is simply perfect.

1 slice of sourdough bread

1 tablespoon (14 g) mayonnaise

1 slice of sharp Cheddar cheese

½ of a sausage link, cooked and sliced

1 large egg, cooked sunny side up

Salt and pepper, to taste

Chopped fresh parsley, for garnish

Toast the bread to your liking and spread with the mayonnaise. Place the Cheddar cheese slice on top, followed by the cooked sausage slices. Top with the fried egg and season with salt and pepper to taste. Garnish with freshly chopped parsley.

Yield: 1 serving

Watermelon Radishes
and Crème Fraîche

‗‗‗‗

I have this habit of buying produce simply because of its beauty. As you can imagine, when I first laid eyes on a watermelon radish, I fell in love. Their bright pink center lends a stunning color to this recipe, and luckily enough, they taste great. If you can't find this particular variety, rest assured that any type of radish will work just as well.

Tip
―――
Crème fraîche is a lovely thickened cream that is both tart and buttery. If you can't find it, using a smaller amount of sour cream will work just as well.

2 slices of sperlonga or country bread

3 tablespoons (45 g) crème fraîche

8 to 10 thin slices of watermelon radish

6 to 8 sprigs of watercress

Maldon sea salt and pepper, to taste

Toast the bread to your liking and spread a layer of crème fraîche over each slice. Divide the radish slices between the slices of toast, and scatter each with a few sprigs of watercress. Season with Maldon sea salt and pepper to taste.

Yield: 2 servings

Salami and Havarti

There are many times throughout the day when I simply need a snack—something not too heavy, but filling enough to hold me over until my next meal. Well, this recipe does just that. I love the tanginess that the whole-grain mustard lends to this recipe; it gives this snack a little extra kick and pairs so nicely with the smooth and mild flavor of the Havarti cheese.

1 slice of shepherd's bread

1 teaspoon whole-grain mustard

1 slice of Havarti cheese

3 or 4 slices of salami

1 or 2 cornichon pickles, thinly sliced

Toast the bread to your liking. Spread the whole-grain mustard over the toast and top with the Havarti cheese and salami slices. Garnish with the sliced cornichon pickles.

Yield: 1 serving

Peanut Butter and Banana

—

When I was a little girl, my mom would often make me peanut butter and banana sandwiches, which were always drizzled with just the right amount of honey. To this day, it remains a classic flavor combination that I still enjoy, especially with the addition of toasted walnuts.

1 slice of honey wheat bread

2 to 3 tablespoons (32 to 48 g) creamy peanut butter

½ of a banana, thinly sliced

1 tablespoon (8 g) chopped walnuts, toasted

Honey, for drizzling

Toast the bread to your liking and spread with a layer of peanut butter. Top with the sliced banana, a sprinkle of the chopped walnuts, and a drizzle of honey.

Yield: 1 serving

Vanilla Bean Greek Yogurt and Kiwi

The pleasant brightness of kiwi is a beauty to behold, especially in the colder months. And while I can't always decide how to use them, this recipe does the trick. Greek yogurt provides a tangy bite, while the kiwis lend their signature tartness.

1 slice of honey wheat or white bread

2 to 3 tablespoons (30 to 45 g) vanilla bean Greek yogurt

6 slices of kiwi

1 tablespoon (5 g) shredded coconut

Agave, for drizzling

Toast the bread to your liking and spread a layer of vanilla bean Greek yogurt on top.

Top with the sliced kiwi, shredded coconut, and a light drizzle of agave.

Yield: 1 serving

Spicy Chorizo and Scrambled Egg

Growing up, my mother would often make me scrambled eggs for breakfast, although I frequently considered it an extra special day when chorizo made an appearance on my plate. This recipe is essentially that childhood meal, just prepared on a warm piece of toast. The addition of the chipotle peppers in the cream lends a wonderful smoky flavor that ties everything together, so drizzle your toast with a little or a lot.

⅓ cup (35 g) Mexican or veggie chorizo

1 teaspoon vegetable oil

1 large egg, beaten

Salt and pepper, to taste

1 of slice sourdough or wheat bread

Chipotle Cream (right)

A few sprigs of cilantro, for garnish

Queso fresco, for garnish

Chipotle Cream

1 cup (230 g) sour cream

2 chipotle peppers, canned in adobo sauce

1 to 2 teaspoons chipotle sauce from can, to taste

2 teaspoons lime juice

Salt to taste

Place all the ingredients in a blender and purée until smooth, adding salt to taste. Place the Chipotle Cream in a small bowl and set aside.

Yield: 1 cup (230 g)

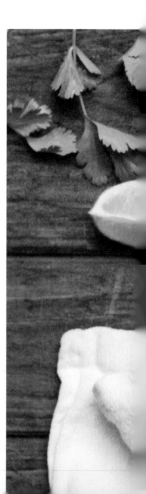

Tip

Queso fresco is a wonderfully moist and mild-flavored Mexican cheese. It's a choice garnish that adds another layer of flavor to this dish. If you're looking for a substitute, try using a mild feta cheese.

Dice the chorizo and place in a small 7-inch (18 cm) skillet set over medium heat. Cook the chorizo until firm and crumbly. Remove from the pan and set aside.

Wipe out the pan and set over medium-low heat. Add the vegetable oil and once hot, pour in the beaten egg and scramble to your liking. Season with salt and pepper to taste.

Toast the bread to your liking then place the warm chorizo over the top. Place the egg on top of the chorizo and drizzle with the Chipotle Cream. Garnish with the fresh cilantro and queso fresco.

Yield: 1 serving

Panfried Ham and Eggs

I don't think there is a more classic breakfast combination than this one. I decided to mix it up and panfry my ham before putting it on my toast. I really love the texture of the crisp ham contrasted with the tender fluffiness of scrambled eggs; there couldn't be a better way to start the day.

2 to 3 teaspoons (10 to 15 ml) vegetable oil

4 thin slices of maple ham

1 slice of sourdough bread

2 tablespoons (28 g) mayonnaise

1 teaspoon sriracha, or more to taste

2 large eggs, scrambled

1 teaspoon fresh chopped chives, for garnish

In a small dish, mix together the mayonnaise and sriracha and set aside. Add oil to an 8-inch (20 cm) skillet pan and set to medium-high heat. Once the oil is hot, fry the ham until lightly browned and crispy.

Toast the bread to your liking then spread a layer of the spicy mayonnaise over the toast. Top the toast with the scrambled eggs and fried ham and garnish with chives.

Yield: 1 serving

Spinach and Leek Scramble

My sister-in-law once made a delicious egg bake for the holidays that was filled with fresh winter vegetables and herbs. I loved it so much that I wanted to make a toast version of it for myself. This recipe only takes a few minutes to make, but it tastes like it could have taken all morning.

2 teaspoons olive oil

3 tablespoons (17 g) thinly sliced leeks

¼ teaspoon minced garlic

⅓ cup (10 g) chopped spinach

2 large eggs, beaten

Salt and pepper, to taste

1 slice of semolina or country bread

1½ tablespoons (23 g) crème fraîche

Chopped fresh chives, for garnish

Set a small 8-inch (20 cm) skillet over medium heat and add the olive oil. Once hot, add the leeks and sauté until tender, about 1 to 2 minutes. Add the minced garlic and chopped spinach and continue to cook just until the spinach wilts. Turn down the heat slightly and then add the beaten eggs. Scramble the eggs to your liking, seasoning with salt and pepper to taste.

Toast the bread to your liking and spread a layer of crème fraîche over the top. Place the scrambled eggs on top and garnish with the chives.

Yield: 1 serving

Tip

This recipe also works quite well with whole wheat bread.

Cream Cheese and Orange Marmalade

I love cream cheese on bagels, so I thought why not try it on my toast? I can't tell you how many mornings I run out the door without a bite of breakfast, which I am aware is not the best thing to do. That is why I love a simple recipe like this. Not only is it easy to put together, but it is also quite satisfying when you don't have enough time to make a proper breakfast.

1 slice of white or brioche bread

1 to 2 tablespoons (15 to 30 g) cream cheese, softened

2 to 3 teaspoons (13 to 20 g) orange marmalade

1 tablespoon (8 g) dried cranberries

Toast the bread to your liking and spread on a layer of cream cheese, followed by a layer of orange marmalade. Sprinkle the dried cranberries over top.

Yield: 1 serving

Warm Lentils and Crispy Pancetta

During the colder months, I often crave warm and filling dishes. Hearty soups begin to frequent the dinner table, hot chocolate is my drink of choice, and my love for lentils is reawakened.

The warm, crispy pancetta mixed with freshly cooked lentils in this recipe makes a meal that will warm you from the inside out.

1 teaspoon olive oil, plus more for drizzling

2 tablespoons (10 g) diced pancetta

½ of a clove of garlic, minced

¼ cup (50 g) cooked lentils

1 tablespoon (15 ml) balsamic vinegar

1 tablespoon (15 ml) water

A few sprigs of fresh dill

Salt and pepper, to taste

1 slice of shepherd's or multigrain bread

Handful of arugula

1 fried egg, cooked to your liking

Chile flakes, for garnish

Pink Himalayan salt, to taste

Tip

This recipe also works quite well with whole wheat bread.

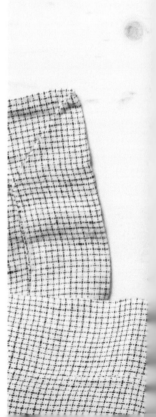

Set a small 8-inch (20 cm) skillet over medium heat and add the olive oil. Once hot, add the pancetta and sauté until crispy, about 3 to 4 minutes. During the last minute, add the minced garlic and cooked lentils and cook for an additional 2 minutes or until the lentils are warmed through.

Remove the lentils from the pan and, with the heat still on, add the balsamic vinegar and water to the skillet, scraping up any brown pieces at the bottom of the pan. Continue to cook until the liquid is reduced by half and then pour it over the lentils. Toss the lentils with a few sprigs of fresh dill, seasoning with salt and pepper to taste.

Toast the bread to your liking. Toss the arugula with a light drizzle of olive oil and place on top of the toast, followed by the warm lentils and the fried egg. Garnish with chile flakes and a pinch of pink Himalayan salt.

Yield: 1 serving

Roasted Butternut Squash and Goat Cheese

Oh boy, do I remember the first time I cut my own butternut squash. It definitely took a bit of work, but the payoff was more than worth it. Luckily, many stores sell presliced squash, which is a great option if you are short on time. This squash is such a warm and inviting fruit, and when roasted, it possesses a sweet and pleasant flavor.

5 ounces (140 g) butternut squash, cut into ¼- to ½- inch (6 mm to 1.3 cm) cubes

1 teaspoon olive or grapeseed oil

Salt and pepper, to taste

2 slices of multigrain or sourdough bread

¼ cup (56 g) goat cheese, softened

Fresh sage leaves, chopped, for garnish (optional)

Preheat the oven to 400°F (200°C, or gas mark 6). Place the butternut squash on a baking sheet lined with parchment paper and drizzle with the oil, tossing to coat.

Season with salt and pepper to taste and bake for 15 minutes or until fork tender and slightly charred.

Toast the bread to your liking and spread each slice with a layer of goat cheese. Divide the roasted squash between the slices and garnish with the freshly chopped sage.

Yield: 2 servings

Sliced Pears with Honey Butter

The sweet smell of cinnamon fills my home as the winter months begin. And one of my favorite ways to incorporate this spice is to mix it in with my butter, always with a bit of honey added. This creates a delicious, intriguing spread that can be used on everything during this time of year, especially on this toast! I recommend toasting your bread without any butter or oil, and instead slathering on a satisfying amount of honey butter once your bread is toasted.

1 slice of multigrain or seeded bread

1 tablespoon (17 g) Honey Butter (right)

½ pear, thinly sliced

1 tablespoon (8 g) chopped walnuts, toasted

Honey, for drizzling

Toast the bread to your liking and allow to cool slightly before spreading with a layer of the softened Honey Butter. Top with the sliced pear, chopped walnuts, and a drizzle of honey.

Yield: 1 serving

Honey Butter

½ cup (112 g) unsalted butter, softened

¼ cup (80 g) honey, or more to taste

½ teaspoon ground cinnamon

Pinch of salt

Place the butter in a stand mixer fitted with the paddle attachment and beat until softened. Add the honey, cinnamon, and salt, mixing until fully combined. Place the softened butter on a piece of parchment paper and roll into a log shape, twisting the ends to seal.

Store in the refrigerator until ready to use.

Yield: ¾ cup (200 g)

Pepperoni and Garlic Crostini

—

Sometimes I find myself craving a big slice of pizza, but I try not to give into that urge too often. Instead, I turn to this trusty recipe that is packed with everything that I would want on a pizza anyway. Make it as a small snack for yourself or for a large gathering of friends; either way, everyone will be happy.

16 baguette slices, cut diagonally ½-inch (1.3 cm) thick

Olive oil, for brushing

1 or 2 large cloves of garlic, sliced in half

32 slices of pepperoni

14 to 16 small balls of buffalo mozzarella

Chopped fresh basil, for garnish

Balsamic glaze, for drizzling

Preheat the oven to 375ºF (190ºC, or gas mark 5). Brush the baguette slices with olive oil on both sides and place on a baking sheet.

Toast for 8 to 10 minutes, or until golden brown, making sure to turn halfway through the baking time. Once out of the oven, rub a cut garlic clove half on each baguette slice.

Place 2 slices of pepperoni on each baguette slice and then slice each mozzarella ball into thirds and place 3 or 4 slices on top. Garnish with a bit of chopped fresh basil and a drizzle of balsamic glaze.

Yield: 16 servings

Roast Beef and Swiss Tartine

When I want a sandwich, I typically prefer to have more filling than bread, and that's why I love a simple yet satisfying open-faced sandwich like this one. I start with a bit of spicy horseradish mayo and layer it with Swiss cheese, tomatoes, and roast beef for a delightful meal.

2 tablespoons (28 g) mayonnaise

1 teaspoon horseradish, or to taste

1 small ciabatta square, sliced in half

2 large slices of Swiss cheese

8 slices of tomato

8 or 10 slices of roast beef

Handful of arugula

Olive oil, for drizzling

Kosher salt and pepper, to taste

In a small dish, stir the mayonnaise and horseradish together; set aside.

Toast the ciabatta to your liking and then spread a layer of the horseradish mayo over each slice.

Place the Swiss cheese slices over the mayo, followed by the tomato slices and roast beef. Toss a handful of arugula with a bit of olive oil, seasoning with Kosher salt and pepper to taste, and place on top; cut in half before serving.

Yield: 2 servings

Sautéed Rainbow Chard and Tomatoes

Rainbow chard is an extremely beautiful and vitamin-rich vegetable. I really enjoy cooking with this leafy green not only for its flavor, but also for its beauty. Be sure to try this recipe if you are looking for a healthier way to enjoy your toast.

1 tablespoon (15 ml) olive oil

3 tablespoons (30 g) diced yellow onion

1 clove of garlic, minced

5½ ounces (155 g) rainbow chard, chopped with stems intact

5 cherry tomatoes, quartered

1 teaspoon red wine vinegar

Salt and pepper, to taste

2 slices of French or garlic bread

2 poached eggs

Chile flakes, for garnish (optional)

Set a 10-inch (25 cm) skillet over medium heat and add the olive oil. Once hot, add the diced onion and cook until translucent, about 2 to 3 minutes.

Add the minced garlic and cook for an additional 30 seconds. Add the rainbow chard and cherry tomatoes, stirring occasionally. Cook until the leaves wilt, about 4 to 6 minutes. Add the red wine vinegar and season with salt and pepper to taste.

Toast the bread to your liking and divide the rainbow chard mixture between both slices, placing a poached egg over the top. Garnish with the chile flakes and more salt and pepper if needed.

Yield: 2 servings

Tip

For a recipe on how to poach an egg, see page 102.

Tip

Kalonji, also known as nigella, is very healthy and provides a welcome peppery flavor. If you're looking for a substitution, try black sesame seeds as a way to achieve that lovely crunch.

Raw Beets and Goat Cheese

Only recently have I embraced eating beets raw. In the past, I always found myself roasting them, but lately, I have been craving their natural crunch.

In this recipe, the beets certainly shine, as their earthy flavor ties everything together. The kalonji seeds lend a lovely texture to this dish, making each bite all the more satisfying.

1 slice of sourdough or spelt bread

1 to 2 tablespoons (15 to 28 g) goat cheese, softened

A few micro greens

½ of a beet, thinly sliced

Olive oil, for drizzling

¼ teaspoon kalonji seeds

Kosher salt, to taste

Toast the bread to your liking and then spread a layer of goat cheese over the top. Scatter enough micro greens to cover the goat cheese and then layer on the sliced beets. Drizzle with a bit of olive oil and garnish with a light sprinkle of kalonji seeds and kosher salt to taste.

Yield: 1 serving

Roasted Broccoli and Spicy Garlic Hummus

—

As opposed to steaming or sautéing, roasting broccoli is an easy and delicious means of preparation. When I take this approach, I love to combine the broccoli with a thick and flavorful spread, like hummus. Enjoy this recipe as a snack or just pile on a lot of broccoli and call it a proper meal.

5 ounces (140 g) broccoli florets

1½ tablespoons (23 g) olive oil

2 teaspoons lemon juice

Salt and pepper, to taste

3 slices of French-style bread

⅓ cup (82 g) roasted garlic hummus

Chile flakes, for garnish

Preheat the oven to 400ºF (200ºC, or gas mark 6). Place the broccoli florets on a baking sheet lined with parchment paper and toss with the olive oil and lemon juice to coat. Season with salt and pepper to taste. Place in the oven and bake for 15 minutes or until tender and slightly charred.

Toast the bread to your liking and spread each slice with a layer of roasted garlic hummus. Divide the roasted broccoli among the slices and garnish with the chile flakes.

Yield: 3 servings

Pear Compote and Crème Fraîche

A warm pear compote is a delicious addition to pancakes, oatmeal, and even toast. I love making a recipe like this, especially when I want something with a lot of flavor. The combination of pear and cinnamon with a hint of cardamom makes for a perfectly spiced wintertime staple.

½ cup (120 ml) dry white wine

½ of a vanilla bean, seeds removed

1⅓ cups (215 g) peeled and diced firm but ripe pear

1 tablespoon (13 g) sugar

¼ teaspoon ground cinnamon

⅛ teaspoon ground cardamom

Pinch of kosher salt

2 slices of brioche or honey wheat bread

3 tablespoons (45 g) crème fraîche

2 to 3 tablespoons (22 to 33 g) pomegranate seeds

Set a small saucepan over medium heat and add the white wine and vanilla bean seeds and pod, cooking until the liquid is reduced by half. Once the liquid is reduced, mix in the diced pear, sugar, cinnamon, cardamom, and kosher salt. Bring the mixture to a gentle simmer, adjusting the heat as necessary.

Cook the mixture for about 10 minutes or until the pears are tender and the compote has a syrup like consistency.

Remove from the heat, discard the vanilla bean pod, and transfer the compote to a separate bowl to cool to room temperature.

Toast bread to your liking and spread each slice with a layer of crème fraîche. Divide the pear compote between both slices. Drizzle any remaining syrup over the top and garnish with pomegranate seeds.

Yield: 2 servings

Tip

This compote can be enjoyed warm or cold, so once it has cooled to room temperature, place it in the refrigerator to cool completely.

Baked Brie and Apples

I am a huge fan of all types of cheeses, especially Brie. But baked Brie? That is a whole new experience. And while it can be paired with many things, the addition of crunchy apples, sweet honey, and earthy walnuts proves to be otherworldly.

1 slice of sourdough bread

Butter or olive oil, for brushing

2 small slices of Brie cheese

4 or 5 thin slices of green apple

1½ tablespoons (12 g) chopped walnuts, toasted

Honey, for drizzling

Preheat the oven to 350°F (180°C, or gas mark 4). Brush both sides of the bread with butter or olive oil and place on a baking sheet lined with parchment paper. Place the slices of Brie cheese on top of the toast and place in the oven for 6 to 8 minutes or until the bread is toasted and the cheese has melted.

Remove from the oven and transfer to a plate. Top with the apple slices, chopped walnuts, and a drizzle of honey before serving.

Yield: 1 serving

Whipped Cannellini Spread and Fresh Spinach

I love hummus, but there is a vast selection of other spreads one can make at home, most of which taste excellent on a slice of toast. For this recipe, I made a spread out of cannellini beans, which have a wonderful flavor that pairs well with the fresh chives and garlic. When topped with fresh spinach, this toast is perfection.

1 slice of squaw bread

3 tablespoons (36 g) Cannellini Bean Spread (right)

Small bunch of spinach

4 or 5 grape tomatoes, quartered

Olive oil, for drizzling

Shaved Parmesan cheese, for garnish

Salt and pepper, to taste

Toast the bread to your liking and add a layer of the Cannellini Bean Spread over the top. Toss the spinach and grape tomatoes with a bit of oil and scatter over the spread. Garnish with the shaved Parmesan cheese, seasoning with salt and pepper to taste.

Yield: 1 serving

Tip

Try adding a few tablespoons of toasted pepitas to give this recipe a little extra crunch.

Cannellini Bean Spread

1 can (15 ounces, or 425 g) cannellini beans, rinsed and drained

2 tablespoons (6 g) chopped fresh chives

1½ cloves of garlic

3 tablespoons (45 ml) olive oil

2½ tablespoons (38 ml) lemon juice

Salt and pepper, to taste

Place all the ingredients in a food processor or blender and purée until smooth and creamy. Taste and add more salt and pepper as needed. Place the spread in an airtight container until ready to use.

Yield: 1½ cups (280 g)

Caramelized Onions
and Swiss Cheese

Caramelized onions may sound like a lot of work, but in reality, preparing them in this manner is a relatively hands-off process. Once caramelized, the onions become slightly sweet and very rich and taste simply amazing when covered with melted Swiss cheese. So just think of this as the ideal way to keep warm and cozy in the winter months.

1 teaspoon olive oil

1 medium yellow onion, thinly sliced

2 slices of country or rye bread

2 slices of Swiss cheese

Chopped fresh parsley, for garnish

Set a medium saucepan over medium-low heat and add the olive oil. Add the onion and allow to cook 40 to 50 minutes, stirring occasionally to evenly brown the onions.

Toast the bread to your liking and divide the caramelized onions between both slices. Place a slice of Swiss cheese over the top. Place on a baking sheet lined with parchment paper. Turn on the broiler and broil the slices of toast until the cheese melts. Garnish each slice with the freshly chopped parsley and serve immediately.

Yield: 2 servings

Recipes for

Spring

Strawberries and Crème Fraîche

Ages ago, my father would gather me and my little sister into the car each year and take us to a festival dedicated to the arrival of strawberry season.

We would practically eat our weight in strawberries, reveling in everything from cakes to kabobs. And what I remember from this festival is that it showed me how truly versatile the strawberry can be. So now when spring comes around, strawberries are mixed in my smoothies, tossed in my salads, and stacked on my toast. In this recipe, the tanginess of the crème fraîche blends with the familiar sweetness of the strawberries for a delectable balance.

1 slice of brioche bread

1 to 2 tablespoons (15 to 30 g) crème fraîche

2 or 3 large strawberries, hulled and sliced

2 to 3 teaspoons (5 to 7 g) chopped hazelnuts, toasted

Honey, for drizzling

Pinch of kosher salt (optional)

Toast the bread to your liking and spread with a layer of crème fraîche. Place the sliced strawberries on top, followed by the chopped hazelnuts. Drizzle with a bit of honey and a pinch of kosher salt.

Yield: 1 serving

Tip

Maldon sea salt works really well with this recipe, as it gives bursts of crunchy saltiness that elevate the overall flavor of the toast. If you don't have any on hand, kosher salt will also work.

Boiled Egg and Avocado

Avocado on anything tastes amazing, but avocado on toast? Perfect. This has been gaining popularity over the past few years and for obvious reasons. The creaminess of the avocado becomes a hearty spread that blends well with a rich variety of flavors, especially a boiled egg. This is an easy and straightforward breakfast recipe that I enjoy often, especially when garnished with some of my favorite springtime produce.

½ of an avocado

1 slice of white or rye bread

1 large hard-boiled egg, sliced

1 radish, sliced

Feta cheese, for garnish

A few pea shoots, for garnish

Olive oil, for drizzling

Maldon sea salt and pepper, to taste

In a small bowl, mash the avocado and set aside.

Toast the bread to your liking and spread a layer of the mashed avocado over the top. Top with the sliced egg, radish slices, feta cheese, and pea shoots. Lightly drizzle with olive oil and season with Maldon sea salt and pepper to taste.

Yield: 1 serving

Chicken and
Goat Cheese Tartine

Fresh herb-roasted chicken from the market is a great companion to any sandwich. But in the spirit of adding an extra layer of flavor, I have introduced goat cheese, sun-dried tomatoes, and basil into the mix for this recipe. If you're in the mood for a lovely springtime tartine, look no further.

1 slice of sourdough or country bread

2 tablespoons (28 g) goat cheese, softened

8 to 10 sun-dried tomatoes, oil packed

¼ cup (60 g) shredded roasted chicken

3 or 4 fresh chopped basil leaves, for garnish

Olive oil, for drizzling

Salt and pepper, to taste

Toast the bread to your liking and spread a layer of goat cheese over the top. Remove the sun-dried tomatoes from the oil and scatter them over the toast. Place the roasted chicken on top and garnish with the freshly chopped basil. Drizzle with a bit of oil and season with salt and pepper to taste.

Yield: 1 serving

Tuna Salad Tartine

———

I would often make my sister and me a tuna sandwich for lunch when we were younger, typically preparing it on two pieces of untoasted white bread. Sadly enough, though, by the time I got around to lunch, my sandwich had usually become a soggy mess.

Since then, I have changed my approach and now place my beloved tuna salad on top of a thick, well-toasted slice of bread. Enjoying this as a tartine also allows the tuna to shine alongside a more fitting proportion of bread. And besides, when you're just piling it on, you can have as much as you want.

1 can (5 ounces, or 140 g) albacore tuna, drained

2 tablespoons (30 g) Greek yogurt

1 tablespoon (14 g) mayonnaise

3 tablespoons (23 g) diced celery

2 tablespoons (16 g) diced carrot

Salt and pepper, to taste

2 slices of seeded or squaw bread

Micro greens, for garnish

In a medium-size bowl, mix together the tuna, Greek yogurt, mayonnaise, celery, and carrot until combined. Season with salt and pepper to taste.

Toast the bread to your liking and then divide the tuna salad between both slices. Garnish each slice of toast with a small bunch of micro greens.

Yield: 2 servings

Ricotta and Lemon-Zested Pea Shoots

The beautiful vines of raw pea tendrils are really something to behold on a piece of toast. Whenever I create a recipe, I like to make it not only pleasant in taste but also pleasing to the eye; an enjoyable meal should be able to engage all your senses. For this recipe, I have garnished the pea tendrils with crispy radishes and pickled onions, which add a nice crunch and a kick of flavor to this toast.

¼ ounce (7 g)
pea shoots, washed
and dried

⅛ teaspoon lemon
zest

1 lemon wedge

Olive oil, for drizzling

1 slice of sourdough
or rosemary bread

1½ tablespoons (24 g)
ricotta cheese

Pickled Onions (right)

1 radish, thinly sliced

Maldon sea salt and
pepper to taste

In a small bowl, toss the pea shoots with the lemon zest, a squeeze of lemon juice, and a light drizzle of olive oil.

Toast the bread to your liking and spread with a layer of ricotta cheese. Garnish the toast with the pea shoots, radish slices, and Pickled Onions. Season with Maldon sea salt and pepper to taste.

Yield: 1 serving

Pickled Onions

¾ cup (180 ml) apple
cider vinegar

¼ teaspoon kosher salt

1 tablespoon (13 g) sugar

2 sprigs of thyme

1 teaspoon black peppercorns

1 medium red onion,
thinly sliced into half moons

Combine the vinegar, salt, sugar, thyme sprigs, and peppercorns in a non-reactive saucepan and bring to a boil. Once boiling, add the onion slices, reduce heat, and allow mixture to simmer for 30 seconds.

Remove the pan from the heat and allow the mixture to cool completely before placing it in an airtight glass container. Onions taste better the longer they soak, so wait at least an hour before using. Store in the fridge until ready to use.

Yield: 2 cups (285 g)

Tip

Try swapping out a slice of burrata for the ricotta cheese as another way to enjoy this toast.

Almond Butter and Date

———

I must admit that a couple years ago, I was very hesitant to try a date. But once while I was out with my friend, she ordered some dates wrapped in bacon, and after my first bite, I instantly wished I had tried these sooner. The savory character of the dish highlighted the distinct taste of the fruit, bringing out notes of honey, caramel, and more. So dates, I have found, are quite delicious. And because they are also very sweet, a little goes a long way. That's why I only used one for this recipe, but of course, feel free to add as many as you like!

1 slice of sunflower seed or whole wheat bread

1½ tablespoons (24 g) almond butter

1 Medjool date, pitted and chopped

1½ tablespoons (11 g) chopped walnuts, toasted

Light drizzle of honey (optional)

Toast the bread to your liking and spread a layer of almond butter over the top. Sprinkle with the chopped Medjool date and walnuts and drizzle with a bit of honey.

Yield: 1 serving

Smoked Salmon and Fennel

I tried smoked salmon during my very first visit to Seattle, and while I was hesitant at first, I really enjoyed it. Since then, I have found myself bringing some home from time to time to experiment with its piquant smokiness. I always enjoy it most when a fitting amount is layered with some type of vegetable like fennel. This serves as the perfect lunch for a bright and lovely spring day.

2 slices of batard or levain bread

4 tablespoons (60 g) cream cheese, softened

2 ounces (55 g) thinly sliced fennel

1 teaspoon lemon juice, or more to taste

Olive oil, for drizzling

Salt and pepper, to taste

2 slices of smoked salmon

Fennel fronds, for garnish (optional)

Toast the bread to your liking and spread each slice with a layer of cream cheese. Toss the sliced fennel with the lemon juice and a bit of olive oil, seasoning with salt and pepper to taste. Place the sliced salmon over the top of the cream cheese, followed by the dressed fennel, and garnish with a fennel frond.

Yield: 2 servings

Cherry Compote
and Mascarpone

—

*This is one of my favorite ways to approach toast as
a dessert and for many reasons. The union of creamy
mascarpone cheese and freshly made sweet cherry
compote imparts a satisfaction that is not easily eclipsed.
This compote is also quite easy to make, and while
it surely feels at home with a dollop of yogurt or in a
bowl of oatmeal, it is simply delightful on a thick
slice of warm toast.*

**1 slice of brioche
bread**

**1½ tablespoons (23 g)
mascarpone cheese**

**3 tablespoons (60 g)
Cherry Compote
(right)**

**2 teaspoons sliced
almonds, toasted, for
garnish**

**Ground cinnamon,
for dusting**

Toast the bread to your liking
and spread with a layer of
mascarpone cheese. Place
3 tablespoons (60 g) of either
warm or cooled Cherry Compote
over the top. Garnish with the
sliced almonds and a light
dusting of cinnamon.

Yield: 1 serving

Cherry Compote

1¼ cups (194 g) pitted
sweet cherries

3 tablespoons (45 ml)
orange juice

½ teaspoon lemon juice

1 tablespoon (13 g) sugar

⅛ teaspoon salt

1 tablespoon (15 ml) water

¾ teaspoon cornstarch

Place the cherries, orange
juice, lemon juice, sugar,
and salt in a medium-size
saucepan and simmer over
medium-low heat for about 5
minutes. In a separate bowl,
mix together the water and
cornstarch until no lumps
remain. Once combined, pour
into the saucepan, mixing to
combine. Increase the heat
slightly and cook until thick,
about 2 to 3 minutes. Remove
from the heat and transfer to a
bowl to cool. Store in the fridge
for up to one week.

Yield: 1 cup (320 g)

Strawberry Cream Cheese Toast

As a little girl, I was absolutely in love with strawberry cream cheese. I would smother as much on my bagel as I possibly could or at least as much as my mom would allow! Figuring that the cream cheese of my past probably only used strawberry flavoring, I wanted to create my own from scratch.

And while I used to enjoy this cream cheese on bagels, I am convinced that a freshly toasted piece of buttery bread is its perfect companion.

1 slice of brioche or white bread

2 tablespoons (30 g) Strawberry Cream Cheese (right)

Chopped strawberries, for garnish

Toast the bread to your liking and spread with enough Strawberry Cream Cheese to cover, about 2 tablespoons (30 g). Garnish with a few chopped strawberries.

Yield: 1 serving

*Strawberry
Cream Cheese*

1 cup (230 g) cream cheese

**¾ cup (128 g) chopped
strawberries**

**5 tablespoons (40 g)
confectioners' sugar**

½ teaspoon vanilla extract

Zest of ½ of a lemon

Pinch of salt

Place the cream cheese in
food processor and pulse a few
times until smooth. Add ½ cup
(85 g) of the strawberries,
confectioners' sugar, vanilla
extract, lemon zest, and salt
and purée until smooth. Add in
the remaining ¼ cup (43 g)
strawberries and pulse just a
few times to lightly chop them.
Transfer to a container and
place in the fridge until ready
to use.

Yield: 1½ cups (300 g)

Bacon, Tomato, and Avocado

―――

I had to include an open-faced sandwich like this one, for it is filled with so many lovely toppings that aren't weighed down by that second piece of toast. The key to making a memorable BTA is to use thick slices of bacon, along with a generous amount of mashed avocado. But most important, I think it's the type of bread you use that really makes this sandwich memorable, so I highly recommend taking the extra step and buying a beautiful loaf of artisan bread.

1 slice of sourdough or levain bread

1 tablespoon (15 g) mayonnaise

½ of an avocado, mashed

3 slices of tomato

2 or 3 slices of thick-cut smoked bacon, cooked

A small handful of arugula

Salt and pepper, to taste

Toast the bread to your liking and spread a layer of mayonnaise, followed by the mashed avocado over the top. Arrange the sliced tomatoes on top, followed by the cooked bacon strips. Top with a small handful of arugula and season with salt and pepper to taste.

Yield: 1 serving

Tip

―――

Looking for a heartier lunch? Simply add an egg cooked to your liking.

Chocolate, Coconut, and Pistachios

―――

Once while I was out with my sister we came across a dessert spot that was selling chocolate-dipped coconut bars. The combination was perfectly harmonious, and I knew I had to bring these flavors together again for a dessert recipe of my own. Well, I found that coconut and chocolate reside together deliciously on a slice of thick toast, and even more so with some pistachios to add a bit of crunch. You can think of this as the perfect response to your sweet tooth's call.

1 slice of brioche or white bread

2 tablespoons (37 g) chocolate spread

1 tablespoon (5 g) shredded coconut

2 teaspoons chopped pistachios, toasted

Toast the bread to your liking and then spread a layer of chocolate spread over the top. Sprinkle with the shredded coconut and garnish with the chopped pistachios.

Yield: 1 serving

Rhubarb Compote and Whipped Cream Cheese

Rhubarb is such an interesting fruit. In appearance, its vibrant red stalks are always surprising, and in flavor, its sharp tartness makes it perfect for pies and compotes. And it is this tartness, effortlessly cutting through their accompanying sweetness, that brings such a pleasant experience to this recipe.

1 slice of brioche bread

1½ tablespoons (19 g) whipped cream cheese

3 tablespoons (60 g) Rhubarb Compote (right)

Toast the bread to your liking and spread a layer of whipped cream cheese over the top. Place 3 tablespoons (60 g) of the Rhubarb Compote over the whipped cream cheese and serve immediately.

Yield: 1 serving

Rhubarb Compote

2 cups (244 g) ½-inch (1.3 cm) diced rhubarb

5 tablespoons (65 g) sugar

2 tablespoons (28 ml) fresh orange juice

⅛ teaspoon kosher salt

Place all the ingredients in a medium-size saucepan set over medium heat. Stir the mixture a few times and bring to a boil; lower the heat and bring to a gentle simmer. Cook for 5 to 7 minutes or until the rhubarb is tender and a few whole pieces remain. Remove from the heat and pour into a small bowl to cool to room temperature.

Yield: 1 cup (320 g)

Tip

Serve this compote at room temperature or slightly chilled. It can be stored in an airtight container in the refrigerator for up to 5 days.

Strawberry and Chocolate Hazelnut Spread

It was in Paris that I first enjoyed the delight of fresh strawberries smothered with chocolate hazelnut spread, all wrapped in the warm blanket of a fresh crêpe.

This recipe is my way of bringing that experience into the realm of toast, which is every bit as good. The little baguette slices retain the Parisian experience but in a satisfying bite-size form, making the mixture of chocolate, hazelnut, and strawberry the perfect treat for your next gathering.

12 baguette slices, cut diagonally, ¼- to ½-inch (6 mm to 1.3 cm) thick

Grapeseed oil, for brushing

¾ cup (222 g) chocolate hazelnut spread

12 fresh strawberries, thinly sliced

Preheat the oven to 375ºF (190ºC, or gas mark 5). Brush the baguette slices with grapeseed oil on both sides and place on a baking sheet lined with parchment paper. Toast for 8 to 10 minutes or until golden brown, making sure to flip the baguette slices halfway through.

Allow to cool slightly and then spread a layer of chocolate hazelnut spread over the top. Garnish with freshly sliced strawberries.

Yield: 12 servings

Sautéed Brussels Sprouts and Bacon

When I was younger, I always steered clear of brussels sprouts. But having grown out of the flavor comfort zones of my youth, I now have a fondness for their unique and interesting taste. And when combined with freshly cooked bacon, their earthy bitterness is complemented by a smoky saltiness, an experience made all the better on a slice of toast.

3 tablespoons (45 g) balsamic vinegar

1½ tablespoons (30 g) honey

2 tablespoons (28 ml) water

3 slices of bacon

5 cups (350 g) shredded brussels sprouts

Salt and pepper, to taste

4 slices of semolina or batard bread

4 tablespoons (20 g) grated mizithra cheese

4 eggs, cooked sunny side up

Tip

Mizithra is a mild cheese from Greece that is made from sheep's milk. If you can't get your hands on some, try using freshly grated Parmesan cheese instead.

Whisk together the balsamic vinegar, honey, and water in a small bowl and set aside. In a 10-inch (25 cm) skillet, cook the bacon over medium-high heat until crispy and cooked through. Remove from the heat, chop, and set aside.

Set the pan back over medium-high heat. Add the shredded brussels sprouts and sauté for 5 to 6 minutes or until lightly browned. Add the vinegar mixture to the pan, cover with a lid, and cook until tender, about 5 minutes. Remove from the heat. Toss in the bacon, seasoning with salt and pepper to taste.

Toast the bread to your liking and then divide the brussels sprouts among the slices of toast. Garnish each slice with a light sprinkle of grated mizithra cheese and top with a cooked egg.

Yield: 4 servings

Pea Pesto and Burrata

———

For some reason, I find peas to be the epitome of spring. Maybe it's due to their beautiful green color or maybe that shucking peapods is an activity I naturally associate with spring. Either way, this pesto has the ability to turn a simple pea into something substantial. This recipe is easy to make and will work wonderfully as an appetizer at your next gathering.

15 to 18 baguette slices, cut diagonally, about ½-inch (1.3 cm) thick

Olive oil, for brushing

Pea Pesto (right)

2 large balls of burrata, sliced

Pea shoots, for garnish (optional)

Lemon zest, for garnish (optional)

Salt and pepper, to taste

Preheat the oven to 375ºF (190ºC, or gas mark 5). Brush the baguette slices with olive oil on both sides and place on a baking sheet lined with parchment paper. Toast for 8 to 10 minutes or until golden brown, making sure to turn the baguette slices halfway through the baking time.

Spread a layer of Pea Pesto on each baguette slice and then place a small amount of sliced burrata on top. Garnish each crostini with the pea shoots and lemon zest. Season with salt and pepper to taste.

Store any remaining pesto in the refrigerator.

Yield: 15 to 18 servings

Pea Pesto

10 ounces (280 g) blanched peas

1 clove of garlic, chopped

¼ cup (57 g) pepitas, toasted

1 teaspoon lemon zest

10 fresh mint leaves

2 teaspoons (10 ml) lemon juice

½ teaspoon salt

¼ teaspoon pepper

¼ cup (60 ml) olive oil

Place the cooked peas, garlic, pepitas, lemon zest, fresh mint leaves, lemon juice, salt, and pepper into a food processor and pulse a few times. While the processor is running, slowly pour in the olive oil and continue processing until the ingredients are fully combined. Taste the pesto, adding more salt or pepper if needed. Transfer to a container and set aside.

Yield: 1½ cups (360 g)

Roasted Fennel and Burrata

Fennel is a wonderfully versatile vegetable that can be enjoyed raw, roasted, braised, or grilled. In this recipe, I have roasted the fennel, which caramelizes it and mellows the tastes of licorice and anise to create a sweet and pleasant flavor. I pair it with burrata, which brings the recipe's flavors together and makes for a wonderful toast.

1 medium-size fennel bulb, about 3 inches (7.5 cm) wide

Olive or grapeseed oil, for drizzling

Salt and pepper, to taste

3 slices of shepherd's or rustic bread

1 large ball of burrata, cut into thirds

2 tablespoons (18 g) pine nuts, toasted

Preheat the oven to 400ºF (200ºC, or gas mark 6). Remove the tops of the fennel, reserving a few fronds. Cut the bulb in half from top to bottom, and slice into ½-inch (1.3 cm) thick wedges. Place the slices on a baking sheet lined with parchment paper and drizzle with oil, making sure to coat both sides. Season with salt and pepper and bake for 35 to 40 minutes until fork tender and slightly charred. Be sure to flip the slices halfway through the cooking time.

Remove the fennel from the oven and set aside.

Meanwhile, toast the bread to your liking and divide the fennel among the slices. Place one slice of burrata on each slice of toast, and garnish with the toasted pine nuts, a light drizzle of oil, and a fennel frond.

Yield: 3 servings

Tip

Burrata is a wonderful cheese that is a firm moz-zarella on the outside, with a soft cream-filled center. If unavailable, try using ricotta or cream cheese instead.

Turmeric Egg Salad Tartine

My dad is a pretty big fan of egg salad, but every time he brought some home while I was growing up, I just couldn't take it. Well, I remember the day he finally changed my mind: he gave me some on a slice of sourdough toast. When I tasted the creamy egg salad against the backdrop of crispy, buttery toast, I immediately began to appreciate it. This recipe does just that and tops it off with a few crunchy radish slices.

2 tablespoons (28 g) mayonnaise

1 teaspoon tumeric

⅛ teaspoon cayenne pepper

2 tablespoons (10 g) diced red onion

2 tablespoons (15 g) diced celery

½ teaspoon minced fresh flat-leaf parsley, plus more for garnish

2 hard-boiled eggs

1 slice of buttermilk bread

1 radish, thinly sliced

Salt and pepper, to taste

In a bowl, mix together the mayonnaise, tumeric, cayenne pepper, onion, celery, and parsley. Roughly chop the hard-boiled eggs, fold into the mixture, and then season with salt and pepper to taste.

Toast the bread to your liking and place the egg salad over the top. Garnish with radish slices and the extra minced parsley.

Yield: 1 serving

Tip

If you prefer a creamier egg salad, simply add more mayonnaise or a few tablespoons (45 to 60 g) of Greek yogurt.

Mushroom and Thyme Scramble

Luckily, cremini mushrooms are available pretty much year-round, although I tend to gravitate toward them during springtime. I love their pleasant mild flavor, which pairs so nicely with strong herbs like thyme. Throw in some fresh ricotta cheese, and a traditional scramble is taken to a new level with these mushrooms.

¾ teaspoon butter or olive oil

½ cup (35 g) sliced cremini mushrooms

1 clove of garlic, minced

¾ teaspoon fresh thyme leaves

2 large eggs, beaten

Salt and pepper, to taste

1 slice of Tuscan or country bread

1½ tablespoons (24 g) ricotta cheese

Olive oil, for drizzling

Set an 8-inch (20 cm) nonstick skillet over medium-high heat and add the butter or olive oil. Once hot, add the cremini mushrooms and sauté until soft and cooked through, 2 to 3 minutes. Add the minced garlic and cook for an additional 30 seconds then mix in the fresh thyme.

Turn down the heat to medium-low and pour in the beaten eggs. Scramble the eggs to your liking, seasoning with salt and pepper to taste.

Prepare the toast to your liking and place the egg scramble on top. Garnish with a dollop of ricotta cheese, a light drizzle of olive oil, and a crack of pepper.

Yield: 1 serving

Tip

If you don't have any ricotta cheese on hand, you can also use sour cream as a nice tangy alternative.

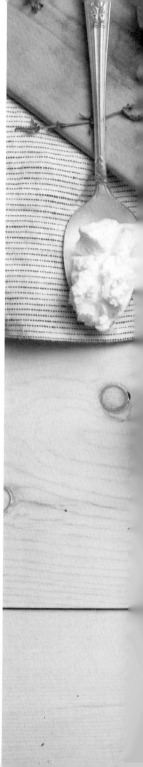

Roasted Cauliflower and Tzatziki

It's quite common for me to buy produce just because I find it beautiful, especially if it's something that I have never tried before. So when I first discovered the bright array of greens and yellows and purples among the ordinarily white cauliflower, I could not resist!

I also found that among all the colors, the taste actually remains consistent. This is entirely fine because the flavor of roasted cauliflower, while being great on its own, is complemented so well by the rest of the ingredients in this recipe. It is so pleasant to prepare and enjoy a meal of such vibrant color and flavor and even more so in springtime.

3 cups (300 g) purple cauliflower florets

1½ tablespoons (23 ml) olive oil

1 clove of garlic, minced

¾ teaspoon ground cumin

2 teaspoons lemon juice

Salt and pepper, to taste

3 slices of country bread

½ cup (120 g) tzatziki

Chopped fresh parsley, for garnish

Preheat the oven to 450°F (230°C, or gas mark 8). In a large bowl, toss the cauliflower florets with the olive oil, minced garlic, cumin, lemon juice, and salt and pepper to taste. Spread the florets evenly onto a baking sheet lined with parchment paper and bake for 15 to 20 minutes until slightly charred and tender.

Toast the bread to your liking and spread each slice with enough tzatziki to cover. Divide the roasted cauliflower among the slices and garnish with a bit of freshly chopped parsley before serving.

Yield: 3 servings

Tip

Tzatziki is a Greek yogurt sauce with sliced cucumbers, garlic, mint, and lemon juice. This sauce adds a lot of flavor to this recipe, but if you need an alternative, you can use some Greek yogurt mixed with a bit of lemon juice and salt to taste instead.

Open-Faced Pastrami Reuben

Sauerkraut is a very interesting condiment. It's one that I don't find myself using too often but that I enjoy when I do. I have combined it with pastrami in this recipe, which introduces a great salty and peppery taste alongside the sourness. I have also brought in pumpernickel, which is a lovely rye bread with a delightful hint of sweetness. The result is pure satisfaction.

1 slice of pumpernickel or marbled rye

1 tablespoon (15 g) Thousand Island dressing

4 or 5 slices of pastrami

2 heaping tablespoons (18 g) sauerkraut

1 large slice of Swiss cheese

Toast the bread to your liking and spread with a layer of Thousand Island dressing. Place the pastrami over the top. Scatter the sauerkraut over the meat, followed by a large slice of Swiss cheese. Place on a baking sheet lined with parchment paper.

Turn on the broiler and broil until the cheese melts. Carefully remove and serve right away.

Yield: 1 serving

Artichokes, Tomatoes, and Cheese

Artichokes are a wonderful vegetable to enjoy in spring. They can be prepared in a variety of ways, although my favorite is when they are marinated. Slightly sour and very tender, marinated artichokes are a satisfying addition to toast, especially when paired with a mild cheese. This recipe is a perfect serving for one, but it can also be enjoyed as an appetizer by splitting multiple servings in half.

1 slice of potato bread

1 garlic clove

4 to 5 wedges of pickled artichoke hearts, room temperature

4 small grape tomatoes, cut into quarters

Salt and pepper, to taste

1½ tablespoons (11 g) shredded mozzarella cheese

Toast the bread to your liking and rub both sides with a clove of garlic that has been cut in half.

Roughly chop the artichokes and scatter over the toast, along with the quartered grape tomatoes. Season with salt and pepper.

Turn the broiler on and sprinkle the mozzarella cheese over the toast. Place on a baking sheet lined with parchment paper and broil until the cheese is melted; serve right away.

Yield: 1 serving

Pineapple and Cottage Cheese

―――

My family and I went to Hawaii a few years ago, and I promise you that I ate an entire pineapple every day. The pineapples were so incredibly tender and sweet that I simply found them irresistible.

In the States, they are pretty easy to find year-round, but they traditionally peak between March and July. The intense sweetness of this fruit always pairs really well with a more mild spread, such as cottage cheese. This perfect balance makes this recipe ideal as a breakfast treat or a lunchtime snack.

1 slice of sourdough or multigrain bread

2½ tablespoons (35 g) cottage cheese

¼ cup (40 g) diced pineapple

2 to 3 teaspoons (10 to 15 g) shredded coconut

Agave, for drizzling

Toast the bread to your liking and spread a layer of cottage cheese over the top. Scatter the diced pineapple over the toast and garnish with the shredded coconut and a light drizzle of agave.

Yield: 1 serving

Panfried Kale and Eggs

―――

Kale is a wonderful, vitamin-rich vegetable that supplies many health benefits, and this recipe takes full advantage of it. Some garlic and lemon juice provide an extra burst of flavor, which comfortably springs forth from the ricotta cheese. I love the extra bit of heat that comes from the cayenne pepper and chile flakes, although feel free to omit one or the other if you prefer a more mild flavor. Once topped with a freshly cooked egg, this really becomes a satisfying meal.

1½ teaspoons olive or grapeseed oil

1 clove of garlic, minced

2 cups (134 g) kale leaves, center stems removed

½ teaspoon lemon juice, or more to taste

Salt and pepper, to taste

Pinch of cayenne pepper

1 slice of multigrain or wheat bread

2 tablespoons (32 g) ricotta cheese

1 egg, cooked sunny side up

Chile flakes, for garnish (optional)

Place the oil in a 10-inch (25 cm) skillet set over medium heat. Once hot, add the minced garlic and cook until fragrant, about 30 seconds. Toss in the kale and lemon juice, stirring to coat. Season with salt, pepper, and cayenne pepper, and cook until the leaves begin to soften, about 1 to 2 minutes. Remove from the heat.

Toast the bread to your liking and spread with a layer of the ricotta cheese. Place the kale on the toast, with a sunny-side-up egg over the top. Garnish with the chile flakes.

Yield: 1 serving

Roasted Carrots
and Hummus

—

Roasting carrots has to be one of the greatest ways to prepare them. Their succulent tenderness makes them a welcomed primary ingredient to this recipe, which can be enjoyed either as a snack or as a full-fledged meal. The flavors of garlic, olive oil, and feta are perfectly complemented by the hummus and in my opinion, best enjoyed on a slice of ciabatta bread.

½ pound (225 g) carrots, washed, dried, and tops trimmed

2 to 3 teaspoons (10 to 15 ml) olive oil

1 clove of garlic, minced

Salt and pepper, to taste

2 slices of ciabatta, about 5½ x 4 inches (14 x 10 cm)

½ cup (123 g) hummus

2 tablespoons (19 g) crumbled feta cheese

Chopped fresh parsley, for garnish

Preheat the oven to 400ºF (200ºC, or gas mark 6). Place the carrots on a baking sheet lined with parchment paper. Rub the carrots with the olive oil and minced garlic, coating well, then season with salt and pepper to taste. Place into the oven and bake for 25 to 30 minutes or until fork tender and slightly charred.

Toast the bread to your liking and spread a layer of hummus onto each slice. Divide the carrots between the slices of toast and sprinkle the feta cheese over each slice. Garnish with the freshly chopped parsley.

Yield: 2 servings

Tip
—

No hummus? Try the Cannellini Bean Spread (page 60) instead.

Asparagus and Poached Eggs

This recipe is for those lazy Saturday mornings when you're happily residing in your favorite pair of pajamas without a care in the world. You might remember that back in the introduction, I spoke of how we're already familiar with meals built on toast, and this is a version of one our classics: eggs Benedict.

Sure, this is not to be categorized under "quick-and-easy" meals, but on a relaxing morning, where do you have to be? And besides, the time and care put into this recipe is what all good meals are made of, and this is definitely worth it. Rather than using the traditional English muffin, I decided to use a hearty slice of sourdough bread on which to present this delightful treat. Go get your second cup of coffee and have some fun.

4 to 5 asparagus stalks, ends trimmed

1 to 2 teaspoons olive oil or butter

Salt and pepper, to taste

1 to 2 teaspoons white vinegar

2 fresh large eggs

1 slice of sourdough bread

⅓ cup (75 g) hollandaise sauce

Fill a large saucepan with water, seasoning generously with salt, and bring to a boil. Prepare an ice bath. Add the asparagus and cook for 3 to 4 minutes or until bright green. Remove from the water, plunge the asparagus into the ice bath for 1 minute, pat dry, and set aside. Reserve the saucepan.

Fill the reserved saucepan with a couple of inches (5 to 7 cm) of water and add the white vinegar; bring to a simmer over medium heat (do not boil).

Crack each egg into a small cup. When the water is hot enough, create a whirlpool by stirring the water in a circular motion. Carefully lower the egg into the water and poach it (untouched) for 2 to 3 minutes for a semisoft yolk and 3 to 4 minutes for a semifirm yolk. Using a slotted spoon, remove the egg from the water and place on a paper towel to soak up any excess water.

Toast the bread to your liking and layer with the cooked asparagus and the poached eggs. Top each egg with a generous amount of hollandaise sauce, seasoning with salt and pepper to taste.

Yield: 1 serving

Once summer arrives, I feel compelled to fill up my schedule with outdoor gatherings, a never-ending flow of ice cream, and multiple trips to the farmers' market. Summer brings about my favorite produce: sweet berries, juicy stone fruit, and vibrant tomatoes. It is truly the perfect time to simplify your meals, allowing you to step away from the oven and instead enjoy all of those beautiful sunsets that only seem to last for a few weeks.

Recipes for

Summer

Tip

Tahini has a very unique taste, but if you are looking for an alternative option, try using a type of nut butter such as cashew.

Honeyed Tahini and Blackberries

Tahini is a wonderful paste made from sesame seeds. It's commonly known for its use in spreads like hummus and baba ghanoush, but it also tastes just as good when sweetened with maple syrup or honey. I prefer spreading a thin layer of this honeyed tahini on my toast and then playing it off against the pleasant tartness of blackberries.

4 tablespoons (60 g) tahini paste

1 tablespoon (20 g) honey, or more to taste

2 slices of honey whole wheat bread

½ cup (75 g) black-berries, cut in half

4 fresh mint leaves, roughly chopped, for garnish

In a bowl, combine the tahini and honey and stir until well blended.

Toast the bread to your liking and divide the sweetened tahini between both slices of toast. Place equal amounts of sliced blackberries over the sweetened tahini and garnish with the freshly chopped mint.

Yield: 2 servings

Whipped Lemon Curd and Summer Berries

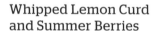

Lemon curd folded into whipped cream is one of the most delightful things to eat. This sweet yet tart cream makes a wonderful partner to the juicy berries that summer yields. I like to think of this as a dessert, but it is also a perfectly acceptable snack to enjoy during any time of the day. I like using a variety of berries, but use whatever kind you fancy the most.

½ cup (120 ml) heavy cream

2½ tablespoons (50 g) lemon curd, or to taste

2 slices of sourdough bread

8 to 10 raspberries

2 or 3 small straw-berries, sliced

In a medium-size bowl, beat the heavy cream until medium soft peaks form. Then fold in the lemon curd with a spatula.

Toast the bread to your liking and allow to cool slightly before dividing the whipped lemon curd and sliced berries between both slices.

Yield: 2 servings

Raspberries and Chocolate

Summertime brings about some of my favorite produce, which of course includes the ever so vibrant and delectably tart raspberry. I love eating them on their own, but just a handful of these tender berries can brighten up any meal or snack. The contrast between the velvety bitterness of the dark chocolate spread and the sharp tartness of the raspberries is perfect, making each bite of this toast feel perfectly indulgent.

1 slice of brioche bread

2 tablespoons (37 g) chocolate spread

¼ cup (31 g) fresh raspberries

Toast the bread to your liking and spread a layer of chocolate spread over the top.

Slice the raspberries in half from top to bottom and scatter over the toast.

Yield: 1 serving

Shaved Cucumber
and Chive Hummus

—

*Every Sunday, I head out to the farmers' market to get
my produce for the week. I look forward to this day because
this is when I get my week's supply of hummus from my
favorite vendor. They always have an interesting array of
flavors that seem to work with anything; feel free to use
whatever you'd like for this recipe. The cucumbers provide
a cool, refreshing crunch, making this toast ideal for a
hot summer day. I like using a mandoline when cutting my
cucumbers, as it helps create uniform slices, but this can
also be achieved by using a sharp knife.*

**2 slices of levain or
seeded bread**

**¼ cup (60 g) chive
hummus**

**2 ounces (55 g)
thinly sliced
cucumber (about
¹⁄₁₆ inch, or 1.5 mm)**

1 lemon wedge

**Salt and pepper,
to taste**

**Chile flakes, for
garnish (optional)**

Toast the bread to your liking
and spread with a layer of chive
hummus over the top. Arrange
enough cucumber slices over
the hummus to cover the toast
and squeeze a bit of lemon
juice on top. Season with salt
and pepper to taste, garnishing
with the chile flakes.

Yield: 2 servings

Tip

Feel free to use any type of hummus that you like, or as an alternative, you can add 1 to 2 tablespoons (3 to 6 g) chopped fresh chives to regular hummus.

Mango and Coconut Whipped Cream

I remember being a bit skeptical at the thought of trying coconut cream, but my first taste totally hooked me. It's silky smooth and delicate and serves as a wonderful alternative for those who cannot have dairy. I prefer the cream lightly sweetened, which creates a lovely base for the vibrant burst of flavor the mango adds to this recipe.

1 slice of brioche or mild sourdough bread

3 tablespoons (30 g) Coconut Whipped Cream (right)

½ of a small yellow mango, sliced

¼ teaspoon chia seeds

Agave, for drizzling

Toast the bread to your liking and allow to cool slightly. Spread 3 tablespoons (30 g) of the Coconut Whipped Cream onto the toast, layering the mango over the top. Sprinkle with the chia seeds and drizzle with a bit of agave.

Yield: 1 serving

Coconut Whipped Cream

1 can (13.5 ounces, or 380 g) coconut milk, refrigerated for 24 hours

½ teaspoon vanilla extract

2½ teaspoons (18 ml) agave, or more to taste

Pinch of salt

Once the coconut milk is properly chilled, carefully open the can and remove the cream that has solidified at the top. Place the cream in a bowl and with a handheld or stand mixer, beat on medium speed until the cream becomes light and fluffy, about 2 to 3 minutes. Add the vanilla extract, agave, and salt, beating to combine.

Yield: 1¾ cups (290 g)

Mascarpone and Berries

―――

Simplicity is a theme I frequently champion in summer, and this recipe is an example of why I do. With just some mascarpone cheese and seasonal berries, this toast can be enjoyed as an early morning pleasure or a midnight snack. You can also have it in your breakfast nook or take it on a picnic; whatever you wish to do, its simplicity will suit your needs.

2 slices of bread of your choice

3 tablespoons (45 g) mascarpone cheese, softened

8 to 10 raspberries

2 tablespoons (18 g) blueberries

2 small strawberries, quartered

Orange blossom honey, for drizzling

Toast the bread to your liking and spread each slice with a layer of mascarpone cheese. In a small bowl, toss the berries together, divide between both slices, and then drizzle with a bit of honey.

Yield: 2 servings

Grilled Zucchini and Halloumi

I used to work at a Greek restaurant, which introduced me to a world of new ingredients and flavors. This is when I became obsessed with grilled halloumi cheese: warm and soft on the inside, delightfully crisp on the outside. I prefer using my panini grill for this recipe, but you can also use a grill pan on the stove top. This cheese is the perfect companion to any assortment of summer veggies, so take your pick and enjoy!

Tip

Whipped garlic spread is a wonderful specialty condiment that is light and smooth and packed with so much flavor. If unavailable, simply rub a cut clove of garlic on each slice of toast as way to achieve that extra layer of flavor.

4 slices of zucchini, ¼-inch (6 mm) thick

Olive oil, for brushing

¼ cup (39 g) corn kernels

2 slices of semolina bread

1½ tablespoons (20 g) whipped garlic spread

2 slices halloumi cheese, about ⅓-inch (8 mm) thick

2 lemon wedges

Chopped fresh parsley, for garnish

Preheat a grill pan over medium-high heat. Brush the zucchini slices with olive oil and place in the hot grill pan. Grill the zucchini slices for about 5 minutes, flipping halfway through or until tender and char marks appear.

Remove the zucchini from the pan and set aside. Add the corn kernels to the pan and cook for a few minutes until charred. Remove from the pan and combine with the zucchini.

Brush the bread with olive oil and toast to your liking. Spread each slice of toast with a thin layer of whipped garlic spread and divide the zucchini and corn between the slices of toast.

Place both slices of halloumi cheese on the grill pan for about 2 minutes, flipping to ensure each side is lightly browned. Place a slice of the grilled halloumi cheese onto each slice of toast and garnish with a squeeze of lemon juice and a bit of freshly chopped parsley.

Yield: 2 servings

Ricotta, Honeydew, and Prosciutto

———

Honeydew melon might seem like an odd ingredient to put on toast, but when paired with crispy prosciutto and fresh ricotta cheese, you might wonder why you didn't try this sooner. This recipe has just the right balance of sweet and salty, which I love on a piece of toast. This works very well as either an enjoyable snack or an appetizer for an intimate gathering.

1 large slice of prosciutto (¾ ounce, or 20 g)

2 slices of country or shepherd's bread

3 tablespoons (48 g) ricotta cheese

6 to 8 thin slices of honeydew melon

Salt and pepper, to taste

Honey, for drizzling

A few sprigs of fresh mint, chopped, for garnish (optional)

Place the prosciutto in a small 8-inch (20 cm) nonstick skillet set over medium heat. Cook for 2 to 3 minutes or until it has become dark and crispy. Remove from the heat and set aside.

Toast the bread to your liking and spread a layer of ricotta cheese over each slice.

Cut the prosciutto in half and place one half on each slice of toast. Divide the melon slices between both slices of toast.

Season with salt and pepper to taste and drizzle with a bit of honey. Garnish with the freshly chopped mint.

Yield: 2 servings

Grape Salad with Ricotta Cheese

———

I have to admit that I have underestimated the true potential of grapes. I love eating them chilled or frozen, but for a long time those were the only two ways I found myself enjoying them. I have since discovered many more ways to incorporate this juicy fruit into my meals, like this lovely grape tartine. The addition of the fresh thyme is delightful, as it imparts a nice earthy balance to the sweet burst of grape you get in each bite. Use any variety of grape to make this salad and enjoy it as a snack or make it as an appetizer for your next summer gathering.

Tip

This is also a wonderful recipe to multiply and make for a larger gathering. Simply toast 12 baguette slices and top each with ricotta cheese and an even amount of grape salad.

¾ cup (114 g) quartered grapes, chilled

¼ teaspoon chopped fresh thyme

2 tablespoons (16 g) chopped walnuts, toasted

1 teaspoon olive oil

½ teaspoon apple cider vinegar

Pinch of salt

4 slices of sourdough or country bread

4 tablespoons (64 g) ricotta cheese

Honey, for drizzling

In a bowl, combine the grapes, freshly chopped thyme, chopped walnuts, olive oil, apple cider vinegar, and salt and set aside.

Toast the bread to your liking and spread an even layer of ricotta cheese over each slice. Divide the grape mixture among the slices of toast and drizzle with a bit of honey.

Yield: 4 servings

Avocado and Chile Flakes

I've loved avocados for as long as I can remember, and there are times I promise you I could eat a couple of them in just one sitting. Avocados have also recently become a very popular accompaniment to toast, which, besides making perfect sense, creates a wonderful canvas for an assortment of toppings. For this recipe, I kept it straightforward and pure, the key here being the addition of lemon salt. This provides an appropriate burst of citrusy goodness that only enhances the already great flavor of the avocado.

1 slice of sourdough or white bread

4 slices of avocado

Olive oil, for drizzling

Pinch of lemon salt

Chile flakes, for garnish

Toast the bread to your liking. Arrange the avocado slices over the toast. Drizzle with a bit of olive oil and sprinkle with the lemon salt and chile flakes to taste.

Yield: 1 serving

Pico de Gallo Eggs

Fresh pico de gallo was a summertime staple in my home growing up and actually still is. It was always the perfect thing to add to tacos, burritos, or pretty much anything else my mom made for dinner. And if by chance some of the pico remained after the evening meal, my mom would toss it into our eggs the next morning. So I came up with my own approach of making these pico de gallo eggs, and it's no surprise that they taste even better with jalapeños and sour cream.

1 tablespoon (15 ml) olive oil or (14 g) butter

2 tablespoons (20 g) diced white onion

2 tablespoons (22 g) diced tomato

2 large eggs, lightly beaten

Salt and pepper, to taste

1 slice of wheat or sourdough bread

2 teaspoons sour cream

½ of a jalapeño, seeded and diced

A few sprigs of fresh cilantro, for garnish

Add the olive oil or butter to an 8-inch (20 cm) skillet set over medium heat. Once hot, add the onion and sauté until translucent, 2 to 3 minutes, and then add the diced tomato and cook for another minute. Reduce the heat slightly, pour in the beaten eggs, and scramble to your liking. Season with salt and pepper to taste.

Toast the bread to your liking and place the scrambled eggs on top. Garnish with the sour cream, diced jalapeño, and a few sprigs of fresh cilantro.

Yield: 1 serving

Tip

If you don't have any lemon salt on hand, try swapping it out for Maldon sea salt and add a squeeze of fresh lemon juice instead.

Heirloom Tomato Tartine

———

With all the amazing produce that summer brings around each year, it's important to enjoy it fully. One of the best ways to do this is through relishing in a simple recipe that celebrates the great natural flavor of some fruit or vegetable. That's what I love about this recipe because it highlights the wonderful taste of tomatoes in their freshest form.

2 large heirloom tomatoes, sliced

4 slices of olive bread

2 cloves of garlic, cut in half

Olive oil, for drizzling

Fleur de sel and pepper, to taste

Slice each tomato into 4 equal slices and set aside.

Toast the bread to your liking and rub a cut garlic clove half on each slice of toast.

Place 2 slices of tomato on each piece of toast and drizzle with olive oil. Season with fleur de sel and pepper to taste.

Yield: 4 servings

Roasted Mixed Berry Jam

Strawberries and raspberries are wonderful summer fruits, and this roasted jam brings them together to create a delicious blend of flavors. Besides, a thick slice of buttery toast lathered with jam is as classic as it gets. The lovely tartness of the raspberries pairs perfectly with the sweetness of the strawberries, making it an ideal companion to a slice of toast.

Tip

This jam can be a bit loose, especially if you use frozen fruit. If you prefer a thicker jam, strain off a bit of the syrup before mashing the berries. Save the extra syrup and drizzle it over some yogurt or ice cream.

1 pound (455 g) strawberries, tops removed

½ pound (225 g) raspberries

½ of a vanilla bean

⅓ cup plus 2 tablespoons (105 g) light brown sugar, packed

2 teaspoons lemon juice

Pinch of kosher salt

1 slice of brioche or wheat bread

Preheat the oven to 350°F (180°C, or gas mark 4). Cut the strawberries in half and add to a medium bowl along with the raspberries. Remove the seeds from the vanilla bean pod and add to the berries, along with the brown sugar, lemon juice, and kosher salt, mixing to combine. Pour the berries into a 10½ inch (27 cm) baking dish, along with the vanilla bean pod.

Place the baking dish in the oven and roast for 1 hour and 15 minutes. Remove the dish from the oven and gently mash the berries with a fork. Allow the jam to cool to room temperature before pouring into a sealed container. Store the jam in the refrigerator for up to 10 to 12 days.

Toast the bread to your liking and spread 2 to 3 tablespoons (30 to 45 g) of the mixed berry jam over the top.

Yield: 1¼ cups (400 g) jam, 1 serving toast

Avocado and Edamame

Smooth and creamy avocado really is toast's best friend, especially when layered with the riches of the season. Edamame has a lovely mellow flavor that perfectly complements the spicy radishes in this recipe. I usually pile my toast to the sky with extra toppings, so start here with this versatile recipe and introduce whatever vegetables you love most.

1 slice of semolina bread

½ of a large avocado

¼ cup (39 g) cooked edamame

1 radish, sliced

Small bunch of micro greens

Olive oil, for drizzling

Salt and pepper, to taste

Toast the bread to your liking. In a small bowl, mash the avocado and spread over the toast. Scatter the edamame and radish slices over the avocado and top with a small handful of micro greens.

Drizzle with a bit of olive oil and season with salt and pepper to taste.

Yield: 1 serving

Parmesan-Roasted Tomatoes with Pesto

———

My mom knew that I wasn't a fan of tomatoes when I was little, but that didn't stop her from trying to change my mind. I guess her persistence paid off because I remember the recipe that eventually won me over; it was her roasted tomatoes topped with cheese. I still love this dish and wanted to turn it into something that could be enjoyed on toast. This recipe is a wonderful way to transform a few tomatoes into a meal that will satisfy anyone.

1 large beefsteak tomato

1 tablespoon (15 ml) olive oil

½ teaspoon minced garlic

½ teaspoon oregano

Salt and pepper, to taste

3 tablespoons (15 g) grated Parmesan cheese

3 slices of country or multigrain bread

3 tablespoons (45 g) pesto

Chopped fresh basil, for garnish

Preheat the oven to 425°F (220°C, or gas mark 7). Slice the tomato horizontally into thirds and place on a baking sheet lined with parchment paper. In a small bowl, mix the olive oil, minced garlic, and oregano and evenly distribute among the tomato slices, seasoning with salt and pepper to taste.

Sprinkle 1 tablespoon (5 g) of Parmesan cheese on each slice and bake for 15 minutes or until tender.

Toast the bread to your liking and spread each slice with 1 tablespoon (15 g) of pesto. Place one tomato slice on top of each piece of toast and garnish with a bit of freshly chopped basil.

Yield: 3 servings

Cherries and Labneh

—

Labneh is a wonderfully thick yogurt that has been strained to create a deliciously creamy texture. This yogurt goes by a few names, the most common of which is Greek yogurt. This is a wonderful spread for toast that can be used for both sweet and savory recipes. Because labneh is quite tart, I like pairing it with sweet cherries, as it creates a perfect contrast of flavors. I've added coconut chips for an extra crunch, but if you don't have any on hand, try using your favorite nut instead.

1 slice of honey wheat or brioche bread

3 tablespoons (45 g) labneh

¼ cup (39 g) cherries, pitted and cut in half

Coconut chips, for garnish

Agave, for drizzling

Toast the bread to your liking and spread a layer of labneh over the top. Scatter the sliced cherries and coconut chips on top and drizzle with agave.

Yield: 1 serving

Peaches and Burrata
with Balsamic Glaze

—

I try to spend as much time outside as possible during the summer. Whether my time is spent in parks, by the water, or just in my backyard, I want to enjoy the sun and its glorious warmth.

Summer is supposed to be easygoing, and I definitely try to reflect this in my meals. For this recipe, I decided to use fresh peaches and creamy burrata cheese as a quick and delicious snack. Not only is this combination of flavors tasty, but this recipe is also incredibly easy to put together.

2 slices of country bread

1 ball of burrata cheese

1 peach, sliced

2 large fresh basil leaves, chopped, for garnish

Maldon sea salt

Balsamic glaze, for drizzling

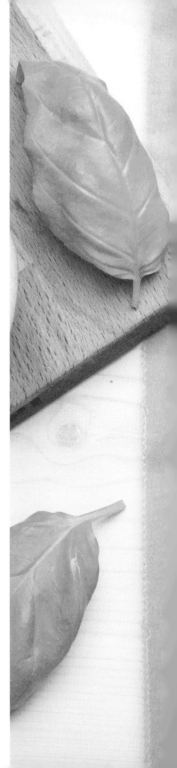

Toast the bread to your liking. Cut the burrata in half, from top to bottom, and place the cheese cut side up onto each slice. Gently spread out the creamy center, covering as much of the bread as possible.

Place 3 or 4 peach slices over the top, enough to cover the toast. Garnish with freshly chopped basil and a pinch of Maldon sea salt. Drizzle the balsamic glaze over the top.

Yield: 2 servings

Green Goddess Tartine

This is a special recipe both for its flavor and for its visual appeal. I wanted to adorn this open-faced sandwich with a thick and flavorful spread, so I created a spicy avocado and feta mixture. The mixture adds to the wonderful ingredients in this toast, making it an incredibly satisfying lunch. And hey, because it's filled with so much summery goodness, you just might want to eat two.

Avocado Feta Spread

2 medium-size avocados
(¾ pound, or 340 g)

⅔ cup (100 g) crumbled feta

½ of a jalapeño, seeded,
or more to taste

1 clove of garlic

2 tablespoons (28 ml)
lemon juice

Salt and pepper, to taste

Place all the ingredients into a food processor and pulse until smooth, adding salt and pepper to taste. Transfer the spread to an airtight container and store in the refrigerator until ready to use.

Yield: 1½ cups (340 g)

1 slice of sourdough bread

Avocado Feta Spread (left)

2 or 3 slices of cucumber

A handful of alfalfa sprouts

2 slices of tomato

Olive oil, for drizzling

Salt and pepper, to taste

Toast the bread to your liking and spread with a layer of the Avocado Feta Spread. Arrange the cucumber slices over the top, followed by the alfalfa sprouts and tomato slices.

Drizzle with a bit of olive oil and season with salt and pepper to taste.

Yield: 1 serving

Tip

If you don't have chocolate chips on hand, try using a premade chocolate spread instead.

S'more Toast

Enjoying a warm, melty s'more has got to be one of the most perfect summer treats. I decided to take the joy of this dessert and turn it into a treat that could be enjoyed on a piece of toast. This recipe might take a bit more effort than a traditional s'more, but it definitely gives this classic delight a run for its money.

2 slices of white or wheat bread

2 tablespoons (22 g) bittersweet chocolate chips

4 large marshmallows

Toast the bread to your liking and then turn on the broiler. Place 1 tablespoon (11 g) of chocolate chips on each slice. Cut each marshmallow along the equator and place 4 slices on each piece of toast. Place on a baking sheet lined with parchment paper.

Place under the broiler and broil until the marshmallows become soft and lightly browned, about 40 to 60 seconds. Remove from the baking sheet and enjoy while warm.

Yield: 2 servings

Maple-Roasted Plums
with Mascarpone

———

Roasting plums is a lovely way to intensify their flavor, and with a drizzling of syrup and a dusting of cinnamon, this recipe becomes richly satisfying. The earthy and herbal qualities of the rosemary appropriately provide a balancing undertone to the sweetness of the plums and combine to make a unique and pleasant dish.

2 medium-size plums (10 ounces, or 280 g)

1½ tablespoons (30 g) maple syrup

2 teaspoons melted butter

⅛ teaspoon ground cinnamon

½ teaspoon roughly chopped fresh rosemary

½ cup (120 g) mascarpone cheese, softened

1½ tablespoons (12 g) confectioners' sugar

¾ teaspoon vanilla bean paste

Pinch of salt

6 slices of sourdough or country bread

Preheat the oven to 400°F (200°C, or gas mark 6). Slice each plum in half and then slice each half into sixths and place in a 2-quart (2 L) baking dish.

In a small bowl, whisk together the maple syrup, melted butter, cinnamon, and freshly chopped rosemary. Drizzle the mixture over the sliced plums, tossing to coat. Place in the oven and roast for 15 to 20 minutes or until tender.

While the plums are roasting, in a small bowl, mix together the mascarpone cheese, confectioners' sugar, vanilla bean paste, and salt until combined.

Toast the bread to your liking and spread a layer of the mascarpone cheese mixture on each slice. Place 4 slices roasted plums on each piece of toast and drizzle with the remaining juices.

Yield: 6 servings

Tip

Vanilla bean paste is available in most stores, but if you can't find any, go ahead and use vanilla extract.

Whipped Ricotta and Blueberries

—

Ricotta is such a versatile cheese. It can be tucked between layers of cheesy lasagna, baked into a cake, or spread over a thick slice of toast with nothing more than a bit of olive oil and a pinch of salt. In the summertime, I like to add a dash of vanilla and lemon zest as a way to liven up the flavor of this beloved cheese. I use blueberries here, but use whatever summer fruit you have on hand; it'll taste just as good.

2 slices of sourdough or white bread

1½ tablespoons (21 g) Whipped Ricotta (right)

½ cup (75 g) fresh blueberries

Lemon zest, for garnish

Honey, for drizzling

Toast the bread to your liking, allowing it to cool slightly before spreading each slice with 1½ tablespoons (21 g) of the Whipped Ricotta. Divide the blueberries between both slices of toast and garnish with the fresh lemon zest and a light drizzle of honey.

Yield: 2 servings

Whipped Ricotta

2 tablespoons (30 g) cream
cheese, softened

¾ cup (188 g) ricotta cheese

3 tablespoons (24 g)
confectioners' sugar

½ teaspoon lemon zest

Pinch of salt

¼ teaspoon vanilla extract

Place all of the ingredients
in a food processor and pulse
until smooth.

Yield: About 1 cup (218 g)

Grilled Peaches and Brie

___

At my local farmers' market, the presence of peaches is the sign that summer has arrived. Peaches are one of my favorite summer fruits; they are so versatile and yet honestly taste amazing when enjoyed on their own. In this recipe, the fruit fuses with the Brie cheese to make a delicious sweet and savory experience. And when presented on crostinis, this makes for the perfect appetizer at a summer gathering. I use either a barbecue or a grill pan to prepare this recipe, both for the peaches and for the bread. Use whatever makes the most sense for you and enjoy!

12 baguette slices,
¼ to ½ inch (6 mm to
1.3 cm) thick

Grapeseed oil, for
brushing

1 medium-size peach,
sliced into 12 equal
pieces

4 ounces (115 g)
Brie cheese

Honey or agave,
for drizzling

12 sprigs of fresh
mint, for garnish

Brush the baguette slices with grapeseed oil and place on the grill or a grill pan set to medium heat; cook until both sides are evenly toasted and char marks appear. Set aside.

Lightly grease a grill or grill pan and set over medium heat. Brush the peach slices with a bit of grapeseed oil and place in the hot grill pan; grill until char marks appear, about 1 to 2 minutes on each side.

Thinly slice the Brie and divide among each baguette slice and top with a warm slice of peach. Garnish each toast with a drizzle of agave and a sprig of fresh mint and serve right away.

Yield: 12 servings

Pineapple, Mint, and Mascarpone

A ripe pineapple never lasts too long in my house. I put it in my smoothies, scatter it over Greek yogurt, or, as of late, grill it to perfection. The sugar in the pineapple caramelizes it a bit, so you are left with an incredible flavorful slice of pineapple to put on a slice of toast. I prefer using mascarpone cheese for this recipe, but cream cheese and crème fraîche are great alternatives.

½ teaspoon honey

½ tablespoon (7 ml) grapeseed oil

3 triangular slices of pineapple, about ½-inch (1.3 cm) thick

1 slice of mild sourdough or white bread

2 tablespoons (30 g) mascarpone cheese

1½ teaspoons chopped macadamia nuts, toasted

Agave, for drizzling

1 or 2 sprigs of fresh mint, chopped, for garnish

Whisk the honey and grapeseed oil together and lightly brush onto the pineapple slices. Lightly grease a grill pan and set over medium heat. Place the pineapple slices in the pan and cook until tender and char marks appear, about 3 to 4 minutes on each side. Remove from the heat and set aside.

Toast the bread to your liking and spread with a layer of mascarpone cheese. Arrange the pineapple slices over the top and sprinkle with the chopped macadamia nuts. Garnish with a drizzle of agave and sprinkle with the freshly chopped mint.

Yield: 1 serving

Greek Toast

This is hands-down one of my favorite salads to make in the summer, and it is no surprise that it tastes just as good when prepared as an open-faced sandwich. I like spreading a thick layer of hummus for the base, followed by layers of fresh summer produce. If you don't have any hummus on hand, a bit of mashed avocado works just as well.

1 rustic panini roll, cut in half (3 x 2 inches, or 7.5 x 5 cm)

4 tablespoons (60 g) hummus

2 slices of tomato

6 slices of cucumber

2 slices of red onion

3 or 4 kalamata olives, diced

2 tablespoons (18 g) crumbled feta cheese

Olive oil, for drizzling

½ teaspoon red wine vinegar

Salt and pepper, to taste

Chopped fresh parsley, for garnish

Toast the bread to your liking. Divide the hummus between both slices of toast, layering the sliced tomatoes and cucumbers over the top. Garnish the toast with the red onion and then sprinkle with the kalamata olives and feta cheese.

Drizzle with a bit of olive oil and ¼ teaspoon of red wine vinegar on each slice. Season with salt and pepper and garnish with a bit of freshly chopped parsley.

Yield: 2 servings

Blistered Tomatoes and Burrata

━━━

Few things surpass the taste of a fresh summer tomato. When they are eaten at their peak of flavor, it's like they've reached a whole new plateau. A longtime favorite snack of mine has been a bowl of slightly firm tomatoes covered with olive oil and salt, but lately I have discovered that blistering tomatoes is another wonderful way to enjoy this fruit. Blistering small tomatoes increases their flavor, and when layered atop some creamy burrata, they make for a delicious summer snack.

Tip

━━━

Balsamic glaze is balsamic vinegar that has been lightly sweetened and cooked down into a syrup. It is a wonderful addition to an assortment of fruits and vegetables. Balsamic vinegar can be substituted if you don't have any glaze on hand.

1 tablespoon (15 ml) olive oil

1 pound (455 g) mini heirloom tomatoes, washed and dried

2 cloves of garlic, thinly sliced

Salt and pepper, to taste

4 slices of wheat or Tuscan bread

2 balls of burrata, cut in half

Balsamic glaze, for drizzling

A few fresh basil leaves, lightly chopped, for garnish

Place the olive oil in a 10-inch (25 cm) pan set over high heat, swirling to coat. Once the oil is hot, add the tomatoes and cook, stirring occasionally, until blistered, about 3 to 4 minutes. Lower the heat slightly, add the sliced garlic, and cook for 1 more minute. Turn off the heat and season with salt and pepper. Transfer to a bowl until ready to serve.

Toast the bread to your liking and top each with a slice of burrata, spreading the creamy center over the toast. Evenly divide the warm tomatoes among the slices of toast. Drizzle each slice with the balsamic glaze and garnish with the freshly chopped basil.

Yield: 4 servings

Grilled Cebollitas and Avocado

Cebollitas, or green onions, make a wonderful accompaniment to steaks and other meat-based dishes, but these flavorful onions are hearty enough to hold their own as the star of this toast recipe. When grilled to perfection, cebollitas are packed with flavor, especially when dressed with lots of fresh lime juice and salt. The outer layers of the onion tend to be a bit tough, so remove those before grilling to ensure a delightful experience.

4 green onions, medium- to small-size bulbs

Olive oil, for brushing

4 slices of country or sourdough bread

1 large avocado, pitted and mashed

4 lime wedges

Salt and pepper, to taste

Chili flakes, to taste

Set a grill pan over medium heat. Remove the roots from the onions and trim the tops so they fit onto each slice of toast once grilled. Brush each onion with olive oil and place on a grill or grill pan set to high; grill for 6 to 8 minutes until tender and charred all around.

Toast the bread to your liking and spread a layer of mashed avocado over each slice. Place a grilled onion on top of each slice. Garnish each toast with a squeeze of lime and sprinkle with salt, pepper, and chili flakes to taste.

Yield: 4 servings

Come September, I am more than ready to welcome fall with arms wide open. Fiery orange and crimson red begin to make their arrival, as the apple orchards and pumpkins patches are filled with the season's best. Cinnamon, cloves, and maple syrup are always within arm's reach, and they taste quite lovely on toast. The recipes in this section are all about comfort and embracing the wonderful produce that comes during this time of year.

Recipes for

Fall

Figs and Mascarpone

I find figs to be an extremely romantic fruit. Their vibrant coloration of either royal purple or bright green is so captivating. When eaten at the right time, figs taste as if they have been soaking in honey for days. With such a sweet flavor to them, figs pair wonderfully with a mild cheese like mascarpone or ricotta. This recipe is an absolute favorite of mine. It's simple, flavorful, and oh so delicious.

1 slice of whole wheat bread

2 tablespoons (30 g) mascarpone cheese, softened

Pinch of ground cinnamon

4 or 5 large slices of fig

1 tablespoon (7 g) chopped hazelnuts, toasted

Honey, for drizzling

Salt, to taste

Toast the bread to your liking. In a small dish, mix together the mascarpone cheese and cinnamon and then spread over the toast. Place the fig slices over the top and sprinkle with the chopped hazelnuts. Garnish with a drizzle of honey and a light sprinkle of salt.

Yield: 1 serving

Tip

You can use either tart or sweet apples for this recipe; both types work wonderfully.

Sliced Apples and Caramel

For the past few years, my husband John and I have set aside a day each fall to drive out to a local apple orchard and bring home a basket of fresh fruit. The local orchard also sells hot caramel cider, warm baked apple pies, and many other treats. Upon arriving home, I always found myself inspired to create some new fall recipe. So I created this toast, which I usually grill in a pan and cover with enough apple slices and caramel to bring out the inner child in anyone.

1 slice of honey wheat bread

½ of an apple, cored and thinly sliced

2 to 3 teaspoons (14 to 21 g) caramel, for drizzling

1 tablespoon (9 g) chopped peanuts, toasted

Toast the bread to your liking and arrange enough apple slices to cover the toast. Drizzle the caramel over the apples and garnish with the chopped peanuts.

Yield: 1 serving

Egg-in-a-Hole

I am sure this breakfast favorite of mine goes by a different name in every household—Egg-in-a-Hole or One-Eyed Pete's? The basic idea here is you butter a piece of bread, punch out a hole in it, and cook an egg right in the middle while you grill it to perfection. It's incredibly simple and incredibly tasty, plus it's a fun way to refresh the way you eat your eggs and toast.

2 teaspoons unsalted butter, softened, plus extra for greasing

1 slice of sourdough or rye bread

1 large egg

Salt and pepper, to taste

¼ cup (37 g) cubed avocado (optional)

Chopped fresh parsley, for garnish (optional)

Spread enough softened butter to cover each side of the bread. Cut out a small hole, about 2 ½ inches (6.4 cm) in diameter, in the center of the bread using the rim of a small cup or jar. Remove the center and set aside.

Set a skillet over medium-low heat and grease with butter. Place the bread in the pan and then crack the egg right into the center. Allow the bottom to cook until golden and the egg has set and then flip and cook the other side. Add the circular cutout and toast until both sides are golden and the egg is cooked to your liking. Season with salt and pepper to taste. Garnish with the cubed avocado and freshly chopped parsley.

Yield: 1 serving

Sunflower Butter and Pear

*Peanut butter, almond butter, sesame seed butter—
you name the nut or seed and I am pretty sure there
is a butter version of it out there. Even though I am
a peanut butter girl at heart, this sunflower butter has
found a welcomed place in my pantry. For this recipe,
I have spread on a thick layer and topped it with fresh
slices of pear; that's my kind of breakfast.*

**1 slice of honey wheat
or seeded bread**

**2 tablespoons (32 g)
sunflower butter**

**½ of a pear, cored and
thinly sliced**

**Ground cinnamon,
for garnish**

Toast the bread to your liking
and spread a layer of sunflower
butter over the top. Arrange
the sliced pears on top to cover
the toast. Garnish with a light
dusting of cinnamon.

Yield: 1 serving

Quince Paste and Manchego

I find quince to be such an interesting fruit. In appearance, it looks like a cross between an apple and a pear, although most varieties are far too sour or tough to be eaten raw, so using these fruits to make a jam or fruit paste is ideal. I wanted to use quince paste as the base for a sweet and savory appetizer. Using a semi-firm version of Manchego cheese is a perfect complement to this fruit paste. This recipe is easy to put together and even easier to eat.

8 baguette slices, cut diagonally, ½-inch (1.3 cm) thick

Olive oil, for brushing

¼ cup (80 g) quince paste

3 tablespoons (18 g) sliced almonds, toasted

1¾ ounces (50 g) Manchego cheese

Preheat the oven to 375ºF (190ºC, or gas mark 5). Brush the baguette slices with olive oil on both sides and place on a baking sheet lined with parchment paper. Toast for 8 to 10 minutes or until golden brown, flipping halfway through the cooking time.

Spread each baguette slice with a layer of quince paste, sprinkling the toasted almonds over the top. Thinly slice the Manchego cheese and divide evenly among the baguette slices, cutting as necessary to fit each slice.

Yield: 8 servings

Maple Raisin Bread with Walnuts

There is no way that I can go through the fall season without buying way too many loaves of raisin bread. It might just be the cinnamon, but there is something I find so comforting when eating a slice of it. This is more of a dessert-type recipe to me, but the added layer of cream cheese makes it a perfectly acceptable breakfast.

1 slice of raisin bread

1 tablespoon (13 g) whipped cream cheese

Maple syrup, for drizzling

1 tablespoon (8 g) chopped walnuts, toasted

Toast the bread to your liking and spread the whipped cream cheese over the top. Drizzle with maple syrup and garnish with the chopped walnuts.

Yield: 1 serving

Rosemary-Roasted Grapes and Ricotta

___

Roasting grapes is a wonderful way to enjoy this beautiful fall fruit. This form of preparation intensifies the flavor of the grapes, which pairs well with the smooth mildness of ricotta cheese. Rosemary and balsamic vinegar lend their unique and present flavors to this recipe, making it truly gratifying.

1 pound (455 g) red seedless grapes

1½ tablespoons (23 ml) grapeseed or olive oil

2 teaspoons balsamic vinegar

1½ teaspoons chopped fresh rosemary

Pinch of salt

4 slices of shepherd's bread

½ cup (125 g) ricotta cheese

Honey, for drizzling

Preheat the oven to 400ºF (200ºC, or gas mark 6). Place the grapes in a large bowl, add the oil, balsamic vinegar, freshly chopped rosemary, and salt, and toss to coat.

Spread the grapes on a baking sheet lined with parchment paper and roast for 10 minutes. Stir the grapes around a bit and continue to roast until they are slightly shriveled and some begin to break down, about 8 to 10 minutes longer.

Toast the bread to your liking and spread each slice with enough ricotta cheese to cover. Divide the grapes and any juices evenly among each slice. Drizzle with honey right before serving.

Yield: 4 servings

Tip

Make this an appetizer by dividing the grapes among 12 to 14 toasted baguette slices, adjusting the ricotta cheese proportion as necessary.

Green Apples and Goat Cheese

▬

This is the perfect recipe to put together for a fall gathering at your home. The creamy tartness of the goat cheese mingles pleasantly with the crispy tartness of the apple. A drizzle of honey and a sprinkle of rosemary release an extra dimension of flavor to the recipe and end up successfully tying everything together.

16 baguette slices, cut diagonally, ¼- to ½-inch (6 mm to 1.3 cm) thick

Softened unsalted butter, for brushing

⅓ cup (75 g) goat cheese, softened

16 slices of green apple

Honey, for drizzling

2 sprigs of fresh rosemary, chopped

Set a skillet over medium-high heat. Brush the baguette slices with the butter on both sides and place in the hot skillet. Toast each side for 2 to 3 minutes or until both sides are golden brown and then remove from the heat.

Spread a layer of goat cheese on each toasted baguette slice and then top each with a slice of green apple. Drizzle with honey and sprinkle with the freshly chopped rosemary before serving.

Yield: 16 servings

Kale Scramble

My love for kale has been touch and go over the past few years, so I am always excited to share a recipe that helps me enjoy this vibrant, vitamin-rich green. I love adding a lot of kale to my scrambles, which usually leaves me with more kale than egg. So, if you prefer a different ratio of eggs to kale, simply reduce the amount of kale slightly. Either way you make it, this healthy scramble over a slice of toast is a great way to start the day.

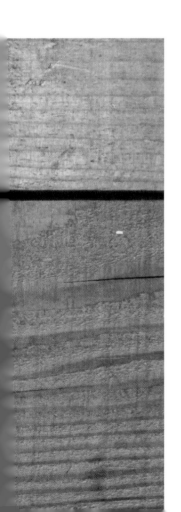

2 teaspoons olive oil

¼ cup (40 g) diced onion

1 clove of garlic, minced

1½ cups (101 g) chopped kale leaves

2 large eggs, beaten

Salt and pepper, to taste

1 slice of bread of your choice

Chile flakes, for garnish (optional)

Set an 8-inch (20 cm) skillet over medium-high heat and add the olive oil. Once the oil is hot, add the diced onion, sauté for 1 minute, and then add the minced garlic and cook until fragrant, about 30 seconds.

Add the kale to the skillet and mix to coat with the olive oil and onions. Sauté the kale until softened, about 2 to 3 minutes.

Turn the heat down to medium and pour the beaten eggs into the skillet. Stir the scramble around a few times until the eggs begin to set. Scramble the eggs to your liking, seasoning with salt and pepper to taste.

Toast the bread to your liking and layer the scramble over the top, along with a sprinkle of chile flakes.

Yield: 1 serving

Crispy Chickpeas and Ricotta

Crispy chickpeas are one of my favorite things to make at home. I like having some on hand because I can toss them into salads or sprinkle them over a toast like this. The unique combination of spicy chickpeas, creamy ricotta cheese, and cool carrots makes for a surprisingly delicious toast, especially because of that lovely crunch.

1 slice of olive or levain bread

2 tablespoons (32 g) ricotta cheese

2 tablespoons (32 g) Crispy Chickpeas (right)

1 large carrot, thinly shaved

Olive oil, for drizzling

Chopped fresh parsley, for garnish

Salt and pepper, to taste

Toast the bread to your liking and spread with the ricotta cheese. Sprinkle 2 tablespoons (30 g) of the Crispy Chickpeas over the top. Arrange enough shaved carrot to cover the toast.

Drizzle with a bit of olive oil and garnish with a generous amount of freshly chopped parsley, seasoning with salt and pepper to taste.

Yield: 1 serving

Crispy Chickpeas

1 can (15 ounces, or 425 g) chickpeas, rinsed and dried

1 tablespoon (15 ml) olive or grapeseed oil

¼ teaspoon garlic salt

⅛ teaspoon pepper

¼ teaspoon cayenne pepper

¼ teaspoon ground cumin

½ teaspoon kosher salt

Preheat the oven to 400°F (200°C, or gas mark 6). In a medium-size bowl, toss the chickpeas with the oil and spices. Spread on a baking sheet lined with parchment paper. Roast for 30 to 40 minutes until crisp, stirring the chickpeas every 15 minutes or so.

Remove from the oven and set aside to cool completely. The chickpeas will remain crunchy for up to a day.

Yield: 1 ½ cups (375 g)

Shredded Chicken and Eggs

This is a recurring lunch staple for me—a thick piece of toast layered with enough toppings to get me through the day. I appreciate a meal like this because it's easy and extremely satisfying. I tend to change the meat around depending on what I have on hand, so feel free to use whatever type of meat you like.

1 slice of wheat or white bread

1 tablespoon (14 g) mayonnaise

3 slices of roma tomato

Small bunch of arugula

¼ cup (60 g) shredded chicken

1 hard-boiled egg, cut into thirds

Olive oil, for drizzling

Salt and pepper, to taste

Toast the bread to your liking and then spread the mayonnaise over the top. Layer on the tomato slices, followed by a small bunch of arugula and the shredded chicken. Place the slices of hard-boiled egg on top and drizzle with a bit of olive oil. Season with salt and pepper to taste.

Yield: 1 serving

Tip

If you don't have any meat on hand, turn this into a veggie sandwich by adding some of your favorite fall produce.

Black Beans and Egg

———

I love adding black beans to my breakfast routine when I have them on hand. They are great in burritos or even as a healthy side for a few scrambled eggs. But believe me when I tell you that some refried beans taste amazing on a crispy piece of toast. I have added a bit of cumin as a way to introduce more flavor and some queso fresco to come alongside as a buttery complement. Fresh beans will certainly taste the best, but canned beans will also work just fine.

2 tablespoons (28 ml) olive oil

1 can (15 ounces, or 425 g) black beans

¾ teaspoon ground cumin

¼ teaspoon garlic salt

1 to 3 tablespoons (15 to 45 ml) water

Salt, to taste

2 slices of wheat bread

Hot sauce, for drizzling (optional)

Queso fresco, for garnish

2 large eggs, cooked sunny side up

Chopped fresh cilantro, for garnish

Add the olive oil to a medium-size saucepan over medium heat. Meanwhile, drain and rinse the beans using a fine-mesh sieve. Once the oil is hot, add the cumin and garlic salt and then add the beans. Using a masher, mash the beans until they become thick and paste-like. Add just enough water to prevent the beans from drying out. Season with salt to taste.

Toast the bread to your liking and divide the mashed beans among the slices. Splash a little hot sauce over the beans and sprinkle with a bit of queso fresco.

Place 1 egg on each slice of toast and season with salt. Garnish with the freshly chopped cilantro.

Yield: 2 servings

Brûléed Cinnamon Toast

There is a great debate on how to make the perfect slice of cinnamon toast. Some like their toast to remain soft, while others prefer theirs a bit crunchy. I happen to be a part of the crunchy camp, but I like using a slightly thicker slice of toast for this recipe because what I really want is a crispy caramelized exterior, but a perfectly soft interior. This approach might take some more time, but you end up with an absolutely delicious slice of cinnamon toast.

6 tablespoons (85 g) unsalted butter, softened

¾ teaspoon ground cinnamon

¼ teaspoon freshly grated nutmeg

½ teaspoon vanilla extract

Pinch of salt

5 slices of buttermilk or sourdough bread

3½ tablespoons (46 g) sugar, divided

Preheat the oven to 350°F (180°C, or gas mark 4). Add the butter, cinnamon, nutmeg, vanilla extract, salt, and 2 tablespoons (26 g) of sugar to a small bowl and mix until combined. Butter each slice of bread on both sides and place on a baking sheet. Bake for 8 to 10 minutes or until lightly toasted.

Garlic Green Beans and Parmesan

—

There are only a few ways that I like to prepare green beans, and this is a favorite of mine. There are a few steps involved, but it leaves you with a crisp green bean that is full of flavor. Piled over toast and garnished with Parmesan cheese, this recipe is sure to please.

6½ ounces (185 g) green beans, ends trimmed

1 tablespoon (14 g) unsalted butter

½ of a shallot, thinly sliced into half-moons

Salt and pepper, to taste

4 slices of rosemary or sourdough bread

1 clove of garlic, cut in half

⅓ cup (67 g) whipped cream cheese

Arugula, for garnish

5 tablespoons (25 g) finely grated Parmesan cheese, for garnish

Fill a 3-quart (2.8 L) saucepan with water and bring to a boil over high heat. Prepare an ice bath. Add the green beans to the boiling water and cook for 2 minutes. Remove from the water and immediately plunge into the prepared ice bath. Leave the green beans in the cold water until no longer warm and then remove and pat dry.

In a medium-size skillet over medium heat, melt the butter. Add the shallot and gently sauté until tender, about 3 to 4 minutes, or until lightly browned. Increase the heat slightly, add the green beans to the skillet, and cook for 3 minutes, seasoning with salt and pepper to taste. Remove from the heat and set aside.

Toast the bread to your liking and rub a cut garlic clove half on each side of the bread. Spread each slice with a layer of whipped cream cheese and top each with an equal amount of green beans. Garnish with a small handful of arugula and finely grated Parmesan cheese.

Yield: 4 servings

Remove the slices from the oven and dust one side with ½ to ¾ teaspoon of the sugar.

Return to the baking sheet. Turn on the broiler and broil each slice of toast until the sugar caramelizes on both sides.

Yield: 5 servings

Honey-Roasted Parsnips

I don't give parsnips the attention they deserve. I actually remember avoiding them as much as possible whenever my mother made them, but they have since grown on me. Parsnips are closely related to carrots and can be prepared in a very similar way. You can choose to make them savory, but in this case I roast them with a bit of honey and fall spices. I particularly like using a slice of wheat or raisin bread for this recipe, but use any kind of bread you have on hand.

4 medium parsnips, peeled

1½ tablespoons (30 g) honey, plus extra for drizzling

1 tablespoon (14 g) unsalted butter

¼ teaspoon ground cinnamon

¼ teaspoon grated nutmeg

Pinch of salt

4 slices of honey wheat or squaw bread

¾ cup (165 g) cottage cheese

Preheat the oven to 375ºF (190ºC, or gas mark 5). Slice each parsnip into fourths and set aside. In a small saucepan over medium heat, melt the honey, butter, cinnamon, nutmeg, and salt together, mixing to combine.

Place the parsnips on a baking sheet lined with parchment paper and drizzle the honey mixture over the top, tossing to coat. Roast for 25 to 30 minutes or until the parsnips are fork tender. Remove from the oven and allow to cool slightly.

Meanwhile, toast the bread to your liking. Divide the cottage cheese among the slices of toast, followed by the roasted parsnips. Drizzle each slice of toast with honey before serving.

Yield: 4 servings

Roasted Pear
with Thyme

Roasted pears are practically a representation of all that is good during fall: rich fruit, sweet maple syrup, aromatic thyme, and smooth vanilla. I like to prepare a batch of these pears when I want a low-maintenance treat, and besides, the roasting process fills my whole house with the aroma of fall.

2 tablespoons (40 g) maple syrup

1 tablespoon (14 g) unsalted butter, melted

1 teaspoon chopped fresh thyme

½ teaspoon vanilla bean paste

1 teaspoon lemon juice

Pinch of salt

1 large Anjou pear, peeled, cored, and cut into 16 slices

4 slices of wheat or multigrain toast

⅓ cup (80 g) crème fraîche

Ground cinnamon, for dusting

Preheat the oven to 375°F (190°C, or gas mark 5). In a small bowl, whisk together the maple syrup, butter, freshly chopped thyme, vanilla bean paste, lemon juice, and salt. Place the pear slices in a 2-quart (2 L) baking dish and drizzle with the maple syrup mixture, tossing to coat. Roast for 30 minutes or until fork tender, basting the pears with the juices once or twice throughout the cooking time. Remove from the oven and allow to cool slightly.

Meanwhile, toast the bread to your liking and spread a layer of crème fraîche and a dusting of cinnamon on each slice.

Top each slice with 4 pear slices and drizzle with any remaining juices.

Yield: 4 servings

Beet and Goat Cheese Salad

I love beets, and this recipe is a wonderful way to showcase their flavor. A natural crowd-pleaser, this light and healthy roasted beet salad toast is ideal for intimate gatherings and outdoor parties. Like every good appetizer should be, this toast is crisply refreshing and packed with flavor.

½ cup (113 g) diced cooked beets

Small handful of arugula

2 tablespoons (16 g) chopped walnuts

¾ to 1 teaspoon olive oil, plus more for brushing

1 teaspoon balsamic vinegar

Salt and pepper, to taste

8 to 10 French baguette slices, ¼- to ½-inch (6 mm to 1.3 cm) thick

⅓ cup (50 g) crumbled goat cheese, for garnish

In a medium-size bowl, combine the cooked beets, arugula, and chopped walnuts. Drizzle with the olive oil and balsamic vinegar, tossing to combine. Season with salt and pepper to taste.

Preheat the oven to 375ºF (190ºC, or gas mark 5). Brush the baguette slices with olive oil on both sides and place on a baking sheet lined with parchment paper. Toast for 8 to 10 minutes or until golden brown, flipping the baguette slices halfway through the cooking time.

Divide the salad evenly among the toasted baguette slices, sprinkling a bit of crumbled goat cheese over the top before serving.

Yield: 8 to 10 servings

Curry Chicken Salad Tartine

I used to pick up a small serving of this salad at my local deli from time to time until I found out how easy it is to make at home. I like making a batch at the beginning of the week so I can have this toast for lunch when I'm short on time. This recipe is flavorful and filling, and it is the perfect lunch whether you're in a rush or not.

3 slices of sourdough or batard bread

¾ cup (36 g) torn romaine lettuce

1 recipe Curry Chicken Salad (right)

3 tablespoons (27 g) chopped peanuts, toasted

3 tablespoons (18 g) chopped scallion, for garnish

Toast the bread to your liking and place a layer of romaine lettuce on each slice of toast. Evenly divide the Curry Chicken Salad among the slices of toast.

Garnish each slice with the chopped peanuts and chopped scallions.

Yield: 3 servings

Curry Chicken Salad

3 tablespoons (45 g) Greek yogurt

2 tablespoons (28 g) mayonnaise

¾ teaspoon curry powder

1 cup (140 g) diced chicken, cooked

⅓ cup (40 g) diced celery

¼ cup (38 g) diced apple

3 tablespoons (27 g) raisins

Salt and pepper, to taste

In a medium-size bowl, mix together the Greek yogurt, mayonnaise, and curry powder until smooth. Fold in the diced chicken, celery, apple, and raisins, seasoning with salt and pepper to taste. If not using right away, store in the refrigerator in an airtight container.

Yield: 1¾ cups (340 g)

Mashed Sweet Potato and Marshmallows

You might look at this recipe and think, sweet potatoes on toast? Really? And I promise you this is one of those recipes that will change your mind as soon as you try it. I found my inspiration from the sweet potato casserole that always makes its appearance during Thanksgiving. So if you're like me and want to enjoy some great holiday meals for more than just one day, this is for you!

1 pound (455 g) sweet potatoes, peeled and sliced into ¼-inch (6 mm) disks

1 tablespoon (15 ml) olive oil

1 tablespoon (20 g) maple syrup, or more to taste

½ teaspoon ground cinnamon

⅛ teaspoon freshly grated nutmeg

Pinch of salt

2 to 3 teaspoons (10 to 15 ml) milk

4 slices of wheat or multigrain bread

¼ cup (112 g) dulce de leche spread

Handful of mini marshmallows

Preheat the oven to 350°F (180°C, or gas mark 4). Place the sweet potato slices on a baking sheet lined with parchment paper and drizzle the olive oil over the top, tossing the slices to coat. Roast for 25 to 30 minutes or until the slices are fork tender.

Carefully remove the slices and place in a medium-size bowl. With a fork or a masher, mash the sweet potatoes until they form a thick paste.

Add the maple syrup, cinnamon, nutmeg, and salt and stir until well combined. If the mixture seems dry, add a few splashes of milk. Set the mixture aside to cool slightly.

Toast the bread to your liking and spread a layer of dulce de leche spread on each slice. Divide the mashed sweet potatoes among the slices of toast, garnishing with enough marshmallows to cover the top of the toast. Place on a baking sheet lined with parchment paper.

Turn on the broiler and place the baking sheet under the broiler; lightly toast the marshmallows for 30 to 45 seconds or until slightly browned. Remove from the heat and serve warm.

Yield: 4 servings

Sautéed Spinach and Egg

Spinach is wonderful addition to any slice of toast, especially when it's sautéed. I like to eat as many greens as I can, and this is an easy way to incorporate some fresh spinach into my breakfast. I like to top this toast off with a soft-boiled egg, but feel free to cook your egg however you like.

1 tablespoon (15 ml) grapeseed or olive oil

1½ tablespoons (15 g) chopped shallot

1 clove of garlic, minced

5 ounces (140 g) spinach

Salt and pepper, to taste

2 slices of sourdough or semolina bread

2 medium soft-boiled eggs

Place the oil in a medium-size skillet and set over medium heat. Add the shallot and cook for 1 minute and then add the minced garlic and cook until fragrant, about 30 seconds. Add the spinach and cook until wilted. Season with salt and pepper to taste.

Toast the bread to your liking and divide the sautéed spinach between the slices of toast. Cut the soft-boiled eggs in half and place 2 halves on each slice of toast.

Yield: 2 servings

Turkey and Cranberry Sauce Tartine

The day after Thanksgiving has always been special to me because it's one of the rare times when leftovers are actually delicious. Everything still tastes good, from the bread to the turkey to—my personal favorite— homemade cranberry sauce. These are all the ingredients you need to make some delicious post-Turkey day toast.

1 slice of multigrain or whole wheat bread

1 tablespoon (15 g) cream cheese, softened

2 tablespoons (32 g) Cranberry Sauce (right)

Small bunch of mixed greens

2 ounces (55 g) sliced turkey breast (about 2 slices)

Salt and pepper, to taste

Toast the bread to your liking and spread with a layer of cream cheese, followed by the 2 tablespoons (30 g) of the Cranberry Sauce. Add a layer of mixed greens, then the turkey slices. Season with salt and pepper to taste.

Yield: 1 serving

Cranberry Sauce

3 cups (300 g) cranberries, fresh or frozen

Zest and juice of ½ of an orange

½ cup (115 g) packed brown sugar

¼ teaspoon salt

½ cup (120 ml) water

To make the cranberry sauce: Place all the ingredients in a medium-size saucepan, stirring to combine, and bring to a gentle simmer. Cook until thick, about 15 to 18 minutes, stirring occasionally. Transfer to a bowl and allow to cool to room temperature before transferring to the refrigerator to cool completely. Store in the refrigerator for up to a week.

Yield: 2 cups (500 g)

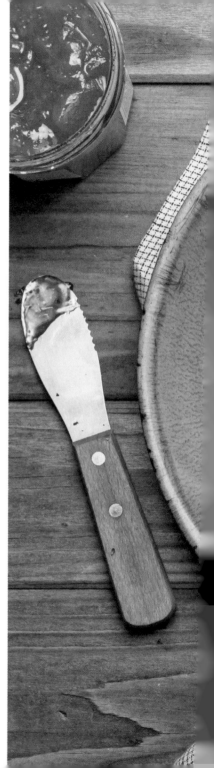

Prosciutto and Fig Jam

I am the kind of girl who loves sweet and salty combinations, and this toast recipe hits the mark. The fig jam complements the saltiness in the most perfect way, all while layered up on a piece of crunchy bread. I like to enjoy something like this when I'm craving a substantial snack, and each time I wonder why I don't eat this more often.

2 slices of shepherd's or country bread

2 tablespoons (40 g) fig jam

3 tablespoons (48 g) ricotta cheese

2 large slices of prosciutto

Freshly ground pepper, to taste

Toast the bread to your liking and spread a layer of fig jam and ricotta cheese on each slice. Top each slice of toast with a piece of prosciutto. Season with a bit of freshly ground pepper before serving.

Yield: 2 servings

Balsamic Meatballs with Mozzarella

*We all crave hearty meals every now and then, right?
Meatballs are one of my go-to comfort foods, and this
open-faced sandwich always hits the spot. A warm, crispy
baguette, covered in marinara sauce, and garnished with
just the right amount of melted cheese: what's not to like?
This meal is a great dinner idea that doesn't take long to
put together—or to completely devour, for that matter.
Keep a fork and knife nearby, just in case.*

**4 baguette slices,
4 x 3 inches (10 x 7.5 cm)**

Butter, for spreading

**1½ cups (368 g)
marinara sauce, heated**

**1 recipe Balsamic Meat-
balls (right)**

**4 slices of mozzarella
cheese**

**Chopped fresh parsley,
for garnish**

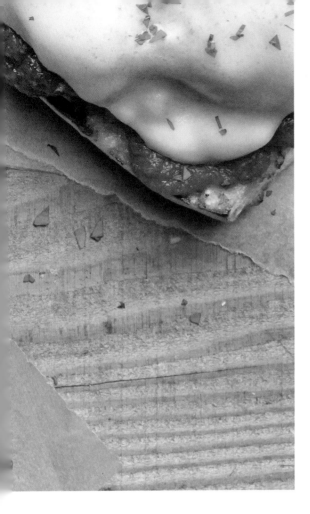

Balsamic Meatballs

1 pound (455 g) ground beef

½ cup (60 ml) milk

¼ cup (30 g) bread crumbs

¼ cup (40 g) diced onions

½ teaspoon salt

¼ teaspoon pepper

1 teaspoon dried oregano

2 teaspoons chopped fresh basil

2 garlic cloves, minced

1½ tablespoons (23 ml) balsamic vinegar

1 large egg, lightly beaten

Preheat the oven to 375°F (190°C, or gas mark 5). In a large bowl, combine the milk and the breadcrumbs and set aside. In another small bowl, whisk together the onions, salt, pepper, oregano, chopped basil, minced garlic, balsamic vinegar, and egg.

Add the ground beef to the bowl with the breadcrumbs and then add the egg mixture. Gently mix all ingredients until fully combined.

Shape about 12 equal golf ball-sized rounds and place on a baking sheet lined with parchment paper. Bake for about 15 to 17 minutes or until the center is no longer pink.

Yield: 12 meatballs

Preheat the oven to 350°F (180°C, or gas mark 4). Butter each baguette slice, place on a baking sheet lined with parchment paper, and toast for 8 to 10 minutes or until toasted to your liking. Once toasted, remove from the oven and preheat the broiler. Top each slice of toast with a few tablespoons of marinara sauce and place 3 meatballs on top. Spoon a bit more marinara sauce over the top of the meatballs, followed by 1 slice of mozzarella cheese.

Place the slices of toast back on the baking sheet and place under the broiler until the cheese has melted, about 1 to 2 minutes. Remove from the heat, garnish with the freshly chopped parsley, and serve right away.

Yield: 4 servings

Croque Monsieur

For our honeymoon, John and I went to Paris, where we both enjoyed our first truly authentic croque monsieur in its city of origin; it was pure bliss. As one of the most famous tartines in existence, the croque monsieur is actually one of the inspirations for this book, as it shows how a satisfying and intricate meal can be built off a single slice of toast. Fresh ham, melted Gruyère, and rich béchamel coalesce and create a truly memorable recipe.

4 slices of white bread

4 teaspoons (20 g) Dijon mustard

1 recipe Béchamel Sauce (right)

8 slices of ham

3 ounces (85 g) Gruyère cheese, thinly sliced

Chopped fresh parsley, for garnish

Toast the bread to your liking and spread 1 teaspoon (5 g) of the mustard on each slice. Then divide half of the Béchamel Sauce among each slice of toast and layer each slice with 2 slices of ham. Divide the remaining Béchamel Sauce over the ham and place a slice of Gruyère cheese on each. Place on a baking sheet lined with parchment paper. Turn on the broiler and broil the toast until the cheese melts. Garnish with the freshly chopped parsley before serving.

Yield: 4 servings

Béchamel Sauce

1 tablespoon (14 g) unsalted butter

1 tablespoon plus 1 teaspoon (11 g) flour

1 cup (235 ml) milk, warmed

½ teaspoon salt

⅛ teaspoon ground pepper, or more to taste

⅛ teaspoon grated nutmeg

¼ cup (20 g) finely grated Parmigiano-Reggiano cheese

Melt the butter in a saucepan over medium heat. Reduce the heat slightly and add the flour. Cook the mixture for 2 minutes, whisking constantly. Slowly pour in the milk and cook the mixture, whisking constantly, until it begins to boil. Once boiling, reduce the heat slightly and allow to cook 1 to 2 minutes or until thick. Remove from the heat and whisk in the salt, pepper, nutmeg, and Parmigiano-Reggiano cheese until well combined.

Yield: 1 cup (235 ml)

Tip

The Béchamel thickens as it cools, so be sure to use it right away.

Baked Eggplant Tartine

When I was a little girl, I once begged my mom to buy me an eggplant because I was convinced there was an egg yolk inside. She bought one for me, and to my disappointment, we found nothing upon cutting it open but a solid interior. Yet my mom cured my disappointment by cooking dinner with the eggplant, and I ended up loving it so much. Since then, I've found that slicing up some eggplant, covering it with bread crumbs, and baking it to crunchy and golden perfection is my favorite way to enjoy it. So this recipe is basically my version of eggplant Parmesan, but on toast. Layers of hot marinara and creamy mozzarella cheese create an open-faced sandwich that is perfect for dinner.

1 pound (455 g) eggplant

¼ teaspoon kosher salt, plus more for sprinkling

½ cup (63 g) flour

¼ teaspoon pepper

2 large eggs, beaten

2 cups (120 g) panko bread crumbs

¼ cup (20 g) finely shredded Parmesan cheese

2 teaspoons dried oregano

2 tablespoons (28 g) softened unsalted butter

7 slices of rosemary or garlic bread

1¾ cups (429 g) marinara sauce, heated

½ cup (60 g) shredded mozzarella cheese

Chopped fresh parsley, for garnish

Cut the eggplant into ½-inch (1.3 cm) slices and sprinkle with a bit of kosher salt on both sides. Place the eggplant slices on a paper towel and let sit for about 30 minutes.

Preheat the oven to 400°F (200°C, or gas mark 6). Gather together 3 medium-size bowls and fill one with the flour and the kosher salt and pepper, another with the beaten eggs, and the third with the panko bread crumbs, Parmesan cheese, and oregano.

Rinse the eggplant slices and pat dry. One by one, dip each slice into the flour mixture, shaking off the excess. Then dip into the egg mixture, letting the excess drip off.

Finally, dip into the bread crumbs. Place the coated slices on a baking sheet lined with parchment paper. Bake for 40 minutes, flipping each slice halfway through the cooking time.

Turn the oven down to 350°F (180°C, or gas mark 4). Butter each slice of bread, place on a baking sheet lined with parchment paper, and toast for 8 to 10 minutes or until toasted to your liking. Once toasted, remove from the oven and preheat the broiler. Top each slice with 3 tablespoons (45 g) of the marinara sauce and 2 slices of roasted eggplant.

Then top each slice with another tablespoon (15 g) of the marinara sauce and a sprinkling of the mozzarella cheese; place back on the baking sheet and place under the broiler until the cheese has melted, about 1 to 2 minutes. Remove from the heat, garnish with the freshly chopped parsley, and serve immediately.

Yield: 7 servings

Index

Acknowledgments

This book would not have been possible without my husband John, to whom I am infinitely indebted. I also want to thank my family, who constantly supported me in whatever way they could. Throughout this whole process, I have always found enriching encouragement from all my friends, and I am deeply thankful for them.

Lastly, I want to thank Jonathan Simcosky, who first invited me to explore the realm of toast and who helped me produce this book.

About the Author

Kristan Raines was only a little girl when she discovered the joy of baking, and it has remained a passion of hers ever since.

She is the creator of *The Broken Bread*, which has been nominated for *Saveur's* Best Food Blog Awards twice, and is a place where she shares her love for seasonal baking and cooking. Kristan has always found food to be a source of joyful activity and fruitful conversation in her life, and she never grows tired of its ability to bring people together and create lasting memories.

She currently lives in Seattle with her lovely husband and works as a freelance recipe developer, food stylist, and photographer.

Also Available

Kitchen Workshop—Pizza
978-1-59253-883-6

Homemade Sausage
978-1-63159-073-3

Global Meatballs
978-1-5923-954-3

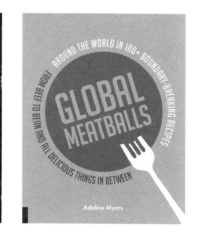